The World of the English Romantic Poets

The endpapers show the Romantic poet in life and in death, as seen by artists painting later in the nineteenth century. Though both pictures are idealized and may be dismissed as 'Shelley ikons', they present valuable evidence of the attitude adopted by society towards the Romantic poet after his death.

The front endpaper is an oil painting by Joseph Severn of *Shelley Writing 'Prometheus Unbound' in the Baths of Caracalla* (1845). The solitary poet communes with nature and the ruins of the classical world; it is in fact true that Shelley did compose his poem in this setting, and his letter to Thomas Love Peacock of 23 March 1819, too long to quote here, is a splendid verbal equivalent of this picture. The painting also suggests thoughts of Mutability and the Revolutions of Empires, themes to which the poet constantly returned. Finally, at a deeper level, the ruins are related to the image of the Labyrinth (page 149) and Shelley's description of the mind of man as 'a wilderness of intricate paths'.

L. E. Fournier's reconstruction of *The Funeral of Shelley: The Last Rite at Viareggio* (Oil. 1889), is reproduced on the endpaper at the back of this book. Trelawny, Leigh Hunt and Byron are beside the pyre; though Leigh Hunt is shown as an old man he was only 38 at the time (August 1822). We need not concern ourselves with the intricacies of Italian law and the regulations governing the disposal of the poet's body after he had been drowned at sea. Nor need we worry too much about what Byron, Trelawny and the others actually did on the real occasion depicted here. What we are looking at is a classical funeral pyre, with all that that implies. Cremation was very unusual in Europe until comparatively recently, and would have seemed pagan if not deliberately anti-Christian. What we see is a small community of the elect witnessing a ceremony of apotheosis; the dead Romantic poet is translated into a higher world than ours. In an age of widespread industrial development and monotonous conformity the Romantic poet is one of the few human beings in touch with the divine; after his death, in an age remarkable for the decline of conventional religious belief—at any rate among the intellectual classes—he will be paid the posthumous honours of a saint.

The World of the English Romantic Poets

A Visual Approach

by **John Purkis**

*The Poet and inspired Maker; who, Prometheus-like,
can shape new symbols, and bring new fire from
Heaven to fix it there.*
Thomas Carlyle

HEINEMANN
LONDON

Heinemann Educational Books Ltd
22 Bedford Square, London WC1B 3HH

LONDON EDINBURGH MELBOURNE AUCKLAND
HONG KONG SINGAPORE KUALA LUMPUR NEW DELHI
IBADAN NAIROBI JOHANNESBURG KINGSTON
EXETER (NH) PORT OF SPAIN

Charlotte's book

British Library Cataloguing in Publication Data

Purkis, John
　　The world of the English Romantic poets.
　　1. Romanticism—England　2. English poetry
　　—19th century　3. English poetry—20th century
　　I. Title
　　821'.8'0914　　　　PR595.R6
　　ISBN 0-435-18735-X

Printed in Great Britain by
BAS Printers Limited, Over Wallop, Hampshire

Contents

Preface

This book contains pictures from the eighteenth and nineteenth centuries, together with a few modern photographs; although the pictures have been collected from many countries and are representative of different styles, they are intended to help the reader of English Romantic poetry. They are not selected for the light they throw on the lives of the poets, nor are they illustrations in the sense that Holman Hunt's *The Eve of St Agnes* derives from the poem by Keats; the aim of the book is to demonstrate pictorially the greater images which appear in the writings of the period.

In an earlier volume of this series—*The World of Shakespeare and his Contemporaries*, by Maurice Hussey—it was possible to draw upon a body of clearly defined visual correspondences which had general currency in the thought of the time; I am thinking of the tradition of the emblem. Unlike the Elizabethan period, the Romantic age was a time of cultural change and shifting values. Imagery had no clear allegorical significance, and it is only by juxtaposing the various places in which an image is used that we can begin to see resemblances and offer interpretations. In making these juxtapositions we have the authority of Shelley, who pointed out that 'the peculiar style of intense and comprehensive imagery which distinguishes the modern literature of England, has not been, as a general power, the product of the imitation of any particular writer.' (Preface to *Prometheus Unbound*). He, of course, attributed it to the all-pervasive Spirit of the Age; but it is certainly true that an amazing number of cross-references between the poets' images are to be found, and certain chapters of this book, such as 'The Voyage of Life' and 'Descent into the Abyss', are attempts to elucidate such chains of imagery.

Although a large quantity of visual material survives, I have not necessarily shown the most famous or obvious picture; in any case, if one thinks of Turner, for example, it must be accepted that a black-and-white reproduction of an oil or water-colour painting can be little more than an *aide-mémoire*. Prints and engravings often illustrate a point more clearly.

In many cases I have gone outside the central period 1795–1824; ideally one would like to show exactly contemporary correspondences, but poetry and painting are not always in step, and it may be necessary to go backwards or forwards forty years in order to demonstrate a particular aspect of poetic consciousness.

Social history is secondary to my main purpose; in fact it must be accepted that the poets of the period are not primarily interested in journalistic descriptions of the world in which they live; as Keats said: 'I feel more and more every day, as my imagination strengthens, that I do not live in this world alone but in a thousand worlds.' As one can see by comparing Keats' letters with his poems, the poet's consciousness appears to be split; living in one world, he dreams of another. But in practice the worlds are linked together, and the pictures may serve to drive the links into a meaningful chain: Cumberland Terrace, John Martin's *Fall of Babylon*, and the palace of Keats' Hyperion, are one such example.

In order to avoid unnecessary confusion, I have kept, after the first chapter, to an approximate chronological narrative; the poets considered are Wordsworth, Coleridge, Byron, Keats and Shelley, and I have tried to find room for allusions to the work of Blake and Clare. Whatever may be the merits of the commentary, I hope that the reader will share in the attempt to decipher the pictures, cryptic as some of them are. It is very much like learning a new language; but I am convinced that, on returning to the poetry of the Romantic period, it will be found illuminating and useful.

J.P.

1 Thomas Banks, Falling Titan (1786). Marble sculpture 85 cm high.
Notice the little figures of the satyr and goats caught up in a catastrophe beyond their control.

1 Overture : Prometheus

The myths of the Greeks have been told over and over again, and they will always retain our interest as stories, even though we cannot be sure of their true interpretation. Perhaps this does not matter; perhaps there is no one meaning. In certain historical periods a particular myth is re-animated because it embodies current human experience; indeed in some cases, and this is a typically Romantic idea, the artist is aware in advance of 'the shadows which futurity casts upon the present'; the date of the sculpture shown opposite (1) is no later than 1786, and is now thought to be 1784. But before we consider the significance of this, listen again to the story of Prometheus, Bringer of Fire.

The Creation of Man

In the first age, when Saturn ruled in Heaven, the world was inhabited by the Titans, or elder Gods. One of these, Prometheus, was a skilful craftsman. He made men by taking earth and water; out of the clay he moulded shapes which, though smaller, resembled those of the gods.

The Golden Age

The first age is also known as the Golden Age. Since the earth produced fruits in abundance, there was no need for ploughing or the building of ships; nor for the weapons of war. Men lived in innocence and happiness, and the season was always Spring.

War in Heaven

Saturn knew that he was fated to be overcome by his children, in the same way that he had supplanted his father, Uranus, before him. So Saturn devoured his children. But one of them, Jupiter, escaped and led a rebellion against his father. The new Gods, the Olympians, took over control of the world. During the fighting the Titans were thrown down and pinned beneath the earth. Prometheus, whose name means Fore-sight, knew who would win; he changed sides and retained his freedom.

The Theft of Fire

These events altered the world for the worse. In the next age, which is known as the Silver Age, the year was divided into seasons of heat and cold. In his anger Jupiter thundered from Heaven, and cared not for the sufferings of men. Prometheus showed mankind how to grow crops and build houses. Out of pity for them he stole fire from Heaven, by lighting a torch at the chariot of the sun. With fire man was able to warm himself in Winter, and to make useful tools and weapons; he was also encouraged by Prometheus to coin money and practise the arts. In this way civilisation began.

The Binding of
Prometheus

In stealing fire Prometheus had disobeyed Jupiter. As a punishment he was chained by Vulcan, Force and Strength (2) to a rock in the Caucasus, a remote region of ice and snow. Every day an eagle, some say a vulture, tormented him by devouring his liver which grew again each night. Prometheus defied Jupiter and would not submit, though he could easily have ended his torture and regained his place in Heaven. For he could see the future, and knew that one day Jupiter would be dethroned by his own child yet unborn; only Prometheus knew who the child's mother would be. This secret he refused to reveal.

This story, which I have tried to make sequential, is extant in several different versions, and it is worth tracing the development of the Romantic image of Prometheus and noticing how parts of the story were amplified or dropped altogether in the fashioning of a new version in which a Romantic artist could discover his own world and his own predicament.

Aeschylus, the first extant Greek dramatist, wrote a trilogy on the subject, of which only the *Prometheus Bound* survives, together with a few fragments of a *Prometheus Unbound*. All this was known to Byron, who seems to have introduced the idea of Prometheus into the minds of Shelley and his wife Mary while they were together in Switzerland in 1816. In one of the later Roman accounts of the story Prometheus was said to have stolen the fire of life to animate his clay-figures. Mary Shelley, combining these hints with a good deal of Gothic horror and Swiss scenery, produced the new myth of *Frankenstein, or the Modern Prometheus*. Frankenstein creates a man ('the monster') with his skill and scientific knowledge. Though it is not made clear, he presumably uses 'electric' fire to animate the body he has put together.

The story did not at first appeal to Shelley at all. This is because in other early Greek versions there are clear references to the use of Fire in offering sacrifices of animals. Shelley was a vegetarian, and seems at first to have regarded Prometheus with abhorrence; by introducing Fire he brought the means to eat meat and so ended the vegetarian Golden Age. Although Shelley was later to make the most radical re-direction of the story, it was left to Byron to hammer out the central Romantic interpretation.

Prometheus is the spirit of revolution, and, at the highest level, of rebellion against the Gods. Jupiter is seen as a tyrant, the upholder of the established order which seemingly cannot be shaken. Poets and artists reject this order; they 'know' the secret of the future which will 'fire' the people and drive kings, priests and other upholders of paternal authority from the earth. Though terrible punishments are inevitable, yet the Romantic spirit is driven to revolt. One day Freedom will be restored, though its advent seems progressively more distant as the years go by.

How a poet could become so alienated from the existing social order will be in part the subject of this book, and I intend at this stage to sketch in the briefest outline. The Prometheus story can be broadly applied to the political events of the period we are studying. For example, the American and French Revolutions can be seen as rebellions against tyrant kings; in the Revolutionary and Napoleonic Wars, which are less simple to justify from any one viewpoint, long-suppressed 'Titanic' forces erupt and human beings lose control of events. Look again at Banks' sculpture (1) and consider how the tiny satyr and his goats will be overwhelmed by the falling rocks. It was as a result of the Napoleonic Wars that historians began to talk of 'historical movements' in which individuals count for nothing; Tolstoy, for example, implies in *War and Peace* that Napoleon was not responsible for the invasion of Russia in 1812.

Even if you do not see what I do in *The Falling Titan*, consider the strange painting by Saint-Ours, usually known in England as *The Greek

11

Earthquake (3). Frightened people are seen fleeing from a violent eruption; a Greek temple is crashing to the ground, and the human beings are powerless to prevent the destruction or, I think, to save themselves. We know from biographical sources that the painter was disturbed by the events succeeding the French Revolution; the earthquake is entirely imaginary, yet obviously had great significance to the artist, who made several versions of the painting. It seems therefore quite reasonable for critics to interpret it as a picture of uncontrollable and cataclysmic disaster, in which established order, works of art and humanity are overwhelmed in the chaos following the Revolution.

A picture like this helps to explain how difficult it is to fit Napoleon into our new myth of Prometheus. He is both a deliverer from the old régime and yet a new tyrant; he builds a new order, yet in spite of all his energy the old order is restored in 1815. As he wasted away on the remote island of St. Helena, he himself said, 'I am nailed to a rock, and a vulture preys on me daily.' Byron made the same comparison in his *Ode to Napoleon Bonaparte*.

At a religious level the story is easily adapted to fuse with Christian ideas. Lucifer, bringer of light, is very close to the concept of the Fire-Bringer. Milton had in any case ennobled Satan in the eyes of the Romantic poets and painters. In John Martin's picture he retains the glory of a fallen archangel (4). This is the heroic figure of *Paradise Lost* Books i and ii, with 'courage never to submit or yield'. Blake observed that 'Milton was of the devil's party without knowing it', and in his own mythological works his heroes rebel against Urizen, the tyrant-God who keeps men in mental chains.

It was Byron who brought Prometheus and Satan together, and tried to reincarnate them in himself and in the defiant rebel-heroes of his own poems, such as Manfred and Cain. His poem *Prometheus* begins:

> Titan! to whose immortal eyes
>   The sufferings of mortality,
>   Seen in their sad reality,
> Were not as things that gods despise;
> What was thy pity's recompense?
> A silent suffering, and intense;
> The rock, the vulture, and the chain,
> All that the proud can feel of pain,
> The agony they do not show,
> The suffocating sense of woe . . .   (ll. 1–10)

and continues:

> . . . Thy Godlike crime was to be kind;
> To render with thy precepts less
> The sum of human wretchedness,
> And strengthen man with his own mind;
> And, baffled as thou wert from high,
> Still in thy patient energy,
> In the endurance, and repulse
> Of thine impenetrable Spirit,
> Which Earth and Heaven could not convulse,
> A mighty lesson we inherit . . .   (ll.35–44)

Notice the emphasis upon the endurance of suffering. It is but a short step from this to the hero of Shelley's *Prometheus Unbound*, who is endowed with Christ-like compassion. But the unbinding of Prometheus is another story, which must be left until the end of the book.

This chapter has been allusive, full of hints which the remainder of the story will make clearer. But then this is what an overture is for. What I have tried to establish is the scale of the enterprise and the method—that of pursuing interrelated chains of imagery. In this case the final link is a real overture, by Beethoven; and one may well ask what use a reference to Beethoven can possibly be in a book about the English Romantic poets. There are two reasons: if, as Walter Pater believed, all the arts aspire to the condition of music, then poetry and pictures need to be complemented by the greater dimension of the most Romantic of the arts; secondly, Beethoven is there to proclaim the European context in which English Romanticism flourished. I hope you will find the time to listen to his *Prometheus* music (Opus 43). Shelley heard the overture before he finally left England; it was played on the Apollonicon, an early machine for reproducing music. Beethoven's ballet *Die Geschöpfe des Prometheus* (1801) is mainly concerned with the creation of mankind. But a theme in the finale was used again as the chief subject in the finale of the Eroica Symphony, a work which links Prometheus and Napoleon in its reference to great men. With this music in our ears we can begin to comprehend the spirit of the age.

4 John Martin, Satan Summoning the Rebe Angels. Mezzotint fro Paradise Lost (1827), illustrating Book I, line 300 ff, of John Milton' poem. To the Romantic Satan has become an attractive figure, symbolizing defiance ar revolution from below.

2 The French Revolution

At some time in the early 1780s the historian Edward Gibbon was working on the fourth volume of *The Decline and Fall of the Roman Empire*. At the end of Chapter XXXVIII he paused in his labours, having just described the 'total extinction' of the Roman Empire in the West, and added some 'General Observations' for the benefit of his readers:

> This awful revolution may be usefully applied to the instruction of the present age. It is the duty of a patriot to prefer and promote the exclusive interest and glory of his native country: but a philosopher may be permitted to enlarge his views, and to consider Europe as one great republic, whose various inhabitants have attained almost the same level of politeness and cultivation. The balance of power will continue to fluctuate, and the prosperity of our own or the neighbouring kingdoms may be alternately exalted or depressed; but these partial events cannot essentially injure our general state of happiness, the system of arts, and laws, and manners, which so advantageously distinguish, above the rest of mankind, the Europeans and their colonies.

5 Fall of the Bastille 14 July 1789. Contemporary print.

He could see no reason why a similar catastrophe should ever recur. After a survey of the entire globe he could find no new race of barbarians capable of overwhelming Western Europe. It was true that the 'great republic' was divided into various independent states, but these posed no real threat to each other.

> The abuses of tyranny are restrained by the mutal influence of fear and shame; republics have acquired order and stability; monarchies have imbibed the principles of freedom, or, at least, of moderation; and some sense of honour and justice is introduced into the most defective constitutions by the general manners of the times. In peace, the progress of knowledge and industry is accelerated by the emulation of so many active rivals: in war, the European forces are exercised by temperate and undecisive contests . If a savage conqueror should issue from the deserts of Tartary, he must repeatedly vanquish the robust peasants of Russia, the numerous armies of Germany, the gallant nobles of France, and the intrepid freemen of Britain; who, perhaps, might confederate for their common defence. Should the victorious barbarians carry slavery and desolation as far as the Atlantic Ocean, ten thousand vessels would transport beyond their pursuit the remains of civilised society; and Europe would revive and flourish in the American world, which is already filled with her colonies and institutions.

6 Benjamin R. Haydon, William Wordsworth (1818). Pencil and chalk drawing. Known in the family as The Brigand.

Furthermore—and this is interesting because Gibbon's sombre theme of the fall of empire might have made him a pessimist—he looks forward to a continuing improvement. Such Progress had been made over the last four thousand years that no disaster could eradicate it:

> We may therefore acquiesce in the pleasing conclusion that every age of the world has increased and still increases the real wealth, the happiness, the knowledge, and perhaps the virtue, of the human race.

It is tempting to linger over the ironies of which Gibbon is so unconscious. Nevertheless, the events in France in 1789 must be seen first of all in the light of these sentiments. The Fall of the Bastille (5) and associated events were a step forward; English liberals could sympathise and rejoice with the French, who appeared likely to imitate our own gentlemanly 'Parliamentary' procedures, given time. There were bound to be a few unfortunate excesses when so many abuses needed to be reformed.

The French Revolution dominates the political thinking of the whole Romantic period, and none of our poets will be exempt from its implications. But the only English poet to visit France during the Revolutionary period was William Wordsworth (6). (No early portrait exists, by the way, which would show us Wordsworth at the age of twenty*; in the case of each poet I have tried to pick out the best portrait. I have also tried to select a picture from the years *c.* 1819 so that one can imagine a meeting such as that between Keats and Wordsworth without too much incongruity.)

Wordsworth landed at Calais on 14 July 1790, the first anniversary of the Fall of the Bastille (7), to find the people celebrating with

> songs, garlands, mirth,
> Banners, and happy faces, far and nigh!
> *Sonnet :* 'Jones, as from Calais . . .'

Notice the iconography of the Revolution, in particular the Liberty tree, the Tricolour, and the red cap of liberty on top of the pole. Watching these scenes, Wordsworth felt that a new age had begun, and that human nature had been born again. A chance had come to do something about changing society, instead of merely talking about it. This is the point of the famous 'Bliss was it in that dawn to be alive' meditation, which is to be found in *The Prelude* (1805 Book X ll. 693 ff; 1850, Book XI, ll. 108 ff).

The 1790 visit was really a holiday excursion; Wordsworth and Robert Jones seem to have made the first of the many Romantic 'walking-tours', in this case to Switzerland. In November 1791 Wordsworth returned to France for a stay of over a year. He was supposed to be studying the French language, and after visiting Paris he moved to Orleans and the valley of the Loire; he was soon in love with Annette Vallon, daughter of a surgeon of Blois. From that town Wordsworth wrote on 17 May 1792 to a friend in England:

You will naturally expect that writing from a country agitated by the storms of a revolution, my letter should not be confined merely to us, and to our friends. But the truth is that in London you have perhaps a better opportunity of being informed of the general concerns of France, than in a petty provincial town in the heart of the kingdom itself.

Annette was a Royalist, and represented the values of an older way of life than the new visions of Paris.

Meanwhile, events in the capital became progressively more bloody, and though the numbers actually killed may have been inflated by atrocity stories, the September Massacres caused doubts in the hearts of many liberals. Wordsworth returned to England at the end of 1792, presumably intending to revisit France in the New Year; but the way was barred by happenings beyond his control. The execution of the King (8), 21 January 1793, produced violent anti-French propaganda in England; by the end of the month France had annexed the Austrian Netherlands (Belgium) and declared war on Great Britain on 1 February. In spite of these events Wordsworth continued to believe that the ideals of the Revolution would succeed, even if he began to feel that France, by her policy of foreign conquest and domination, had begun to betray them.

7 Celebrations of the Fê de la Conféderation Française 14 July 1790. Decorations and Illuminations on the Terrain de la Bastille. *Contemporary print. Similar displays were held all over France.*

---

* See F. M. Blanshard *Portraits of Wordsworth* for a complete list; all are reproduced.

8 *James Gillray*, The Blood of the Murdered Crying for Vengeance. *Print published 15 February 1793, showing the execution of Louis XVI, 21 January 1793. The text in the centre ends: By your affection for your own/Wives & Children—rescue mine:—by your love for your Country, by the blessings of that true liberty which you possess,—by the/virtues which adorn the British Crown,—by all that is Sacred, & all this is dear to you—revenge the blood of a Monarch most/undeservedly butchered,—and rescue the Kingdom of France, from being the prey of Violence, Usurpation & Cruelty.*

3 Industry and Society

Wordsworth returned to London, and later in the 1790s lived in Dorset and Somerset before finally settling at Grasmere. As an observer of rural conditions he was distressed by the increase in poverty and the apparent break-up of the family in times of war and famine. But before moving on to this topic we must try to explore the pattern of society in England at that time.

To some readers it may seem obtuse to attempt to see this pattern through the eyes of William Blake (9). But Blake, unlike the other poets in the group we are considering, had to work to earn a living; the same is true of Clare, whom we shall discuss briefly in Chapter 9. In his day-to-day employment as a commercial engraver Blake was part of the industrial process; he was involved in the combination of different events and practices that are lumped together under the heading of 'the industrial revolution'.*

9 *John Linnell*, William Blake at Hampstead (*c. 1825*). *Pencil.*

Albion at the Mill

The industrial Revolution affected every corner of the British Isles in one way or another; it was certainly not confined, as is often thought, to areas of the North and the Midlands, though it is true that the changing of the landscape was more obvious in those parts of the country. The Albion Mills in Southwark (10), built in the mid-1780s by Samuel Wyatt, were in fact the first mills to be powered by steam. They were flour mills, and one should note that though the word 'mill' in Blake's writings is often used metaphorically for any mechanical system or thought-process, what he seems to have had in the forefront of his mind was a machine for grinding corn. When the Albion Mills were built there were already over five hundred flour mills in London; the population of the city, already approximately one million, made it the largest urban community in the world. The earlier mills were quite small affairs; they were powered by water or by the wind, or sometimes driven by horses walking round and round in a ring; each mill contained only one or two grinding wheels.

*Space will not allow more than a brief treatment of a few aspects of the Industrial Revolution. The recent growth of interest in Industrial Archaeology has led to the production of many well-illustrated books, and it should be possible to find a guide to one's own locality.

Inside the Albion Mills an enormous beam engine provided the power; the up-and-down motion was then converted into rotary motion. The plan was eventually to have three steam-engines driving up to thirty grinding wheels, which would work by day and by night. No wonder the windmillers danced for joy when the Albion Mills were destroyed by fire in 1791.

Whether Blake punned on the name of this building—which must have been known to him—is of little importance, though it helps us to see him in a context of the real world about him; in his prophetic book *Jerusalem* Albion is both Britain and the giant of the same name lying pinned on a rock beneath the island. Blake's mythology is admittedly difficult; in his case it is easier to begin with his pictorial works. Consider, for example, *The Ancient of Days* (11). At a simple level this is an illustration to the Bible, showing God the Creator setting his compasses upon the face of the deep; but to Blake this act of creation is the source of all our woe. If one compares other pictures by Blake it becomes fairly

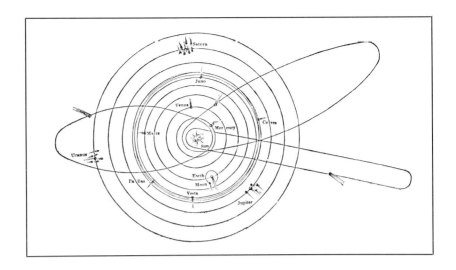

clear from the cramped nature of the figure and the circle in which it is
confined that this is Urizen (a pun upon 'your reason' and 'horizon'), the
God of Death, who has limited our immortal potentiality within the narrow
shell of existence. Just at a time when intellectuals believed that Newton
had driven out superstition and fear by his account of the mathematics of
the Universe (updated in (12)) and the great Architect who had created it, it
was Blake who had the insight that such a limited view of God led to a
limited view of the world and of morality — 'the net of Urizen' — which led
further to the exploitation of men in factories — 'intricate wheels invented,
wheel without wheel'. Furthermore, though he never saw them, he knew
that some of the factories were not intended for peaceful purposes. The
vision of Blake is total; it embraces the whole cosmos, and brings this kind
of insight to bear on the industrial revolution. Consider the pictures 10–12
in relation to this extract from *Jerusalem*:

> Then left the sons of Urizen the plow & harrow, the loom,
> The hammer & the chisel & the rule & compasses; from London fleeing,
> They forg'd the sword on Cheviot, the chariot of war & the battle-ax,
> The trumpet fitted to mortal battle, & the flute of summer in Annandale;
> And all the Arts of Life they chang'd into the Arts of Death in Albion.
> The hour-glass contemn'd because its simple workmanship
> Was like the workmanship of the plowman, & the water wheel
> That raises water into cisterns, broken & burn'd with fire
> Because its workmanship was like the workmanship of the shepherd;

And in their stead, intricate wheels invented, wheel without wheel,
To perplex youth in their outgoings & to bind to labours in Albion
Of day & night the myriads of eternity: that they may grind
And polish brass & iron hour after hour, laborious task,
Kept ignorant of its use: that they might spend the days of wisdom
In sorrowful drudgery to obtain a scanty pittance of bread,
In ignorance to view a small portion & think that All,
And call it Demonstration, blind to all the simple rules of life.

III, folio 65

The Economic Network

An apparent detour into the workings of the pottery industry is now
called for, in order to appreciate the full complexity of the industrial
system and its relation to our poets. Though Josiah Wedgwood (1730–
95) was fully conversant with the whole craft of making a pot, and could
on occasion throw one himself, he saw that the only way to improve
efficiency and accelerate production was to introduce specialization. The
following series of pictures (actually of Enoch Wood's factory), show
clearly the division of labour (13); one can also work out the status of the
various individuals from the plastered or unplastered rooms and the
mode of dress.

13 Scenes from Enoch Wood Representation of the Manufacturing of Earthenware *(1827).*
Broadsheet published by Ambrose Cuddon.

Beating the clay to make it solid, smooth
and pliable fit for the Potter.

First procets of potting is Throwing, forming round
pieces of ware with the Hands and Machine.

Engraving designs on Copper Plates, for producing the much admired "blue printed pots", &c.

Grinding and preparing the various colours for the Enameller or Painter.

"Glazing" or dipping the ware in a prepared liquid, which produces the glossy surface.

A Potters Oven when firing or baking, the ware being therein placed in Safeguards, or "Saggers".

Wedgwood's skill as a designer is what we remember today, and we shall look at an example of his art later (75). It was his care to back up his designs and his factory with a national system of distribution which confirmed his success. His factory, Etruria, was built in 1769 on the bank of the Trent and Mersey Canal, which he had helped to promote; he also involved himself in schemes for road improvement. In this way he could supply his showrooms in London (14); customers could examine the handsome catalogue, engraved on at least one occasion by William Blake

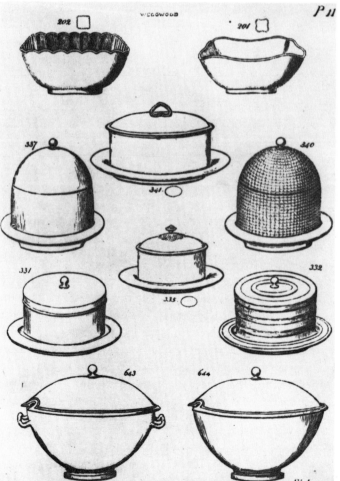

14 *R. Ackermann,* Showrooms of Wedgwood and Byerley, York Street, St. James Square *(1809). Print from the Repository of Arts.*

15 *William Blake, Plate II of the* Wedgwood Catalogue, *showing creamware shapes (1817). Besides the famous designs which we know today— and which brought him little or no money—Blake undertook a variety of commissions such as this in order to earn a living; notice his signature at bottom right. This is his only proven connection with the Wedgwood firm, but it is probable that he worked for them on earlier occasions.*

(15), who was just as much part of the system as the artists in (13) who engrave designs on copper. The whole enterprise supported the Wedgwood family, seen here looking like a passable imitation of the land-owning gentry (16). Two of the sons shown here, Josiah the Younger (centre) and Thomas Wedgwood, used their wealth to assist the arts, and in 1798 gave Coleridge an annuity of £150 a year, providing him with the freedom to write.

Victims

Such an economic system, of which the pottery industry is only one example, enclosed the British Isles and in certain cases the overseas colonies within its net. At a crucial point in the story of *Mansfield Park* Sir Thomas Bertram is despatched to Antigua; Jane Austen was fully aware of his reasons for going. He had to see to the plantations of sugar from which the family's wealth derived. The plantations were worked by negro slaves, and in the eighteenth century a considerable movement of public opinion took place, which ultimately led to the abolition of the slave trade. Blake included 'The Little Black Boy' in *Songs of Innocence* (17), and the poet William Cowper supported the cause. One of its features was a boycott of West Indian sugar.

When Wordsworth returned to England at the end of 1792, he

> found the air yet busy with the stir
> Of a contention which had been raised up
> Against the traffickers in Negro blood. . . .

The Prelude 1805 Book X, ll. 204–6

While he saw the good in this campaign, he still held to the idea that only the success of France in spreading the Revolution would ensure that such a 'rotten branch of human shame . . . Would fall together with its parent tree.' In fact, it was only too easy to feel intense anguish for good causes overseas like West Indian slavery, and ignore the worse cases on one's own doorstep.

Consider 'The Chimney Sweeper' (18) from *Songs of Experience* (1794); it is not my purpose to provide analyses of the poems mentioned, but the ironies here must be brought home. The child is presumably apprenticed, or sold for 'a bit of bread', as Blake put it elsewhere; Church

17 William Blake, The Little Black Boy, *Plates 9 and 10 of* Songs of Innocence *(1789). Etching, then coloured by hand. The first picture shows the boy with his mother, and the second shows the black boy protecting the white boy from the heat and presenting him to Jesus the good Shepherd. The flock can be seen in the background, and the stream and the willow tree are symbols of the landscape of heaven.*

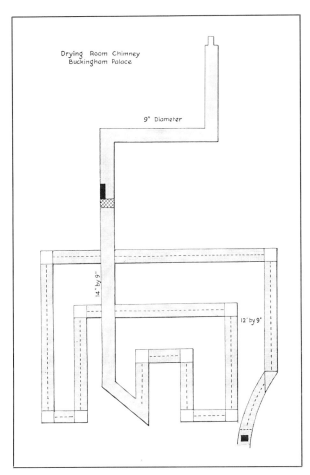

Drying Room Chimney
Buckingham Palace

9" Diameter

14" by 9"

12" by 9"

William Blake, The
imney Sweeper, Plate 37
Songs of Experience
94). Etching, with
our-printing and washes.
ealistic scene: the little
is carrying a bag of
. His blackness stands
against the snow.

Drying Room Chimney,
ckingham Palace.
odern diagram.

and State condone the system which leads to conditions worse than slavery. The children were forced into chimneys like these (19), and those who survived beatings were liable to contract industrial diseases. Little was done about these children for many years, and in 1824 the debate was still 'news' so that James Montgomery reprinted the companion-piece to Blake's poem from *Songs of Innocence* in *The Chimney Sweeper's Friend and Climbing Boy's Album*. Child labour is also illuminated by a reading of Crabbe's 'Peter Grimes' from *The Borough* (1810).

Wordsworth's personal development during the 1790s is complex, but one strand can be followed here. His views on society were for a time influenced by William Godwin, whose *Enquiry Concerning Political Justice* was first published in 1793. Godwin announced that all Man's dreams were within his grasp, and that immense social improvements were possible by the application of reason to morality. Property was to be abolished, and all things held in common. But as a result of his wanderings along the roads of England, Wordsworth abandoned such

20 *Henry Thomson,*
Distress by Land, *(181*
Oil. Shows Stonehenge i
the background. Compar
Wordsworth's mental
picture of a vagrant in T
Prelude *(1805) Book*
VIII, lines 550 ff., or his
encounter with the Fema
Vagrant in 'Guilt and
Sorrow'.

simple solutions. He met so many individual cases of misery that he could no longer believe in general optimism about the future of humanity.

This distressed woman on Salisbury Plain (20) might well be the heroine of Wordsworth's poem of the same name. Notice the grim 'pile of Stonehenge' in the background. Other poets, such as Crabbe and Cowper, had noticed rural poverty; Wordsworth is also concerned with the psychological effects of distress, including madness. 'Guilt and Sorrow: or, Incidents upon Salisbury Plain,' 'The Ruined Cottage',* and many of the *Lyrical Ballads* are about people whose poverty and isolation have stripped them bare of all but the most 'primal' sympathies and passions. Consider, for example, 'The Old Cumberland Beggar' or 'Simon Lee, the Old Huntsman'; Wordsworth treats the subjects of his ballads with such reverence that the intrusions of reality in the first poem are rather unexpected:

> May never HOUSE, misnamed of INDUSTRY,
> Make him a captive!

Because they no longer exist, workhouses have become rather a joke. But they are the logical counterpart of the factory system already described.

Here are the plans for the House of Industry at Onehouse, erected by the fourteen parishes of Stow Hundred in Suffolk in 1781 (21). This is a particularly fine building, and there were the usual protests from ratepayers. Notice the bedrooms for married people on the Chamber Plan (the separation of married couples was a feature of the new Poor Law of 1834). Notice too the self-sufficiency of the community indicated by Woodyard, Cowyard, etc. Obviously there could be many worse examples of a House of Industry, but by illustrating this one I want to emphasize that even a good one is still an extension of a philosophy which sees poverty as a crime — however much better the accommodation shown here might be compared to the cottage or hovel in which the poor person formerly lived.

Attitudes to the Houses of Industry varied. On the one hand, middle-class rate-payers may have felt that it was an extension of the principles of Christian charity to do so much for the sick, the aged and the unemployed. They read the works of political economists, such as Robert Malthus, who answered Godwin's generous visions of the future by pointing out that the population would always outrun food-supply. In any case, it was unsightly to have too many beggars wandering on the roads.

That there were also political reasons for encouraging these establishments is made clear by Thomas Ruggles, a gentleman of Suffolk, in his *History of the Poor*, published in 1794. Houses of Industry are

---

* This later became the First Book of *The Excursion*.

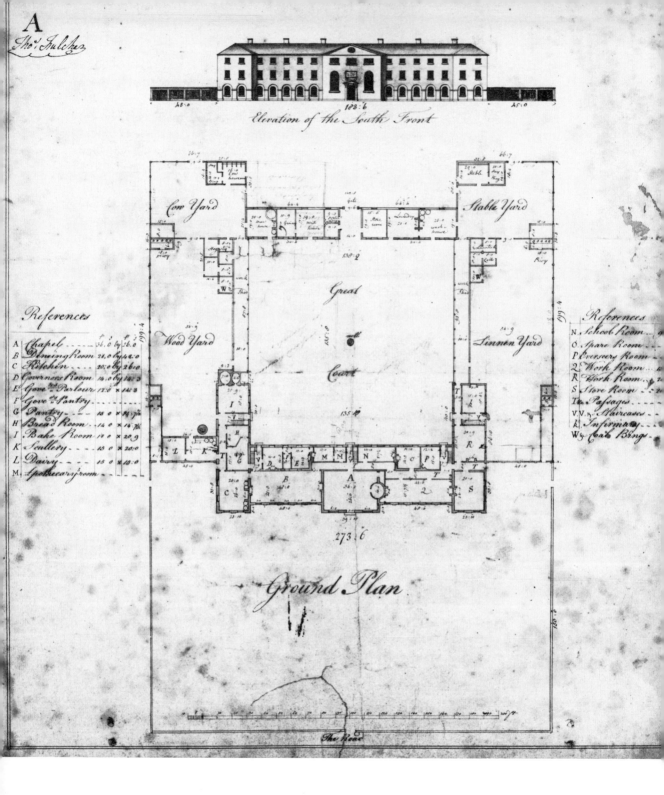

21 Plans of the House of Industry, Onehouse, Stow Hundred, Suffolk, built between 1777 and 1781.

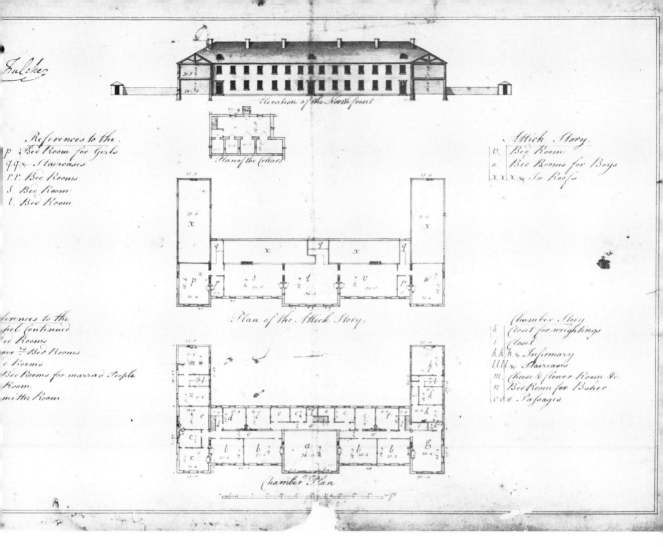

Dulcher

Elevation of the North front

Plan of the Cellar

References to the.
p Bed Room for Girls
q q x Staircases
r r Bed Rooms
s Bed Room
t Bed Room

Attick Story.
v Bed Room
u Bed Rooms for Boys
x x x & In Roofs

Plan of the Attick Story.

References to the
Chapel Continued
Bed Rooms
above 2d Bed Rooms
c Rooms
Bed Rooms for married People
Room
Committee Room

Chamber Story
h Closet for wrightings
i Closet
k k k & Infirmary
l l l x Staircases
m Cheese & flower Room &c
n Bed Room for Baker
o & o Passages

Chamber Plan

recommended as the remedy for most social problems, and in particular 'the unrest of the times' which Ruggles derives from the French Revolution:

the pauper is no longer satisfied with his allowance, nor the labourer with his hire; the faint rumour of distant atrocities, which disgrace human nature, reaches the ear of the multitude cleansed from the blood and carnage, and assumes to them the pleasing shape of liberty and property . . . .

He therefore urges every effort

to establish houses of industry throughout the kingdom; they will present, by anticipation of the cause, a more sure barrier to the insolent attempts of sedition, and the press of democratic violence, than all the barracks in Europe; and they will provide a more secure defence of liberty and property, than the best disciplined standing army.

From this point of view the House of Industry, however hygienic, is a 'concentration camp' for 'undesirable social elements' — to use twentieth-century terms. And it is to Wordsworth's credit that he protests against it.

The argument so far can be summarized as follows. In the 1790s the overthrow of one prison, symbolized by the Bastille, had not in fact secured liberty for all men; Blake saw that scientific and technological progress had led to the construction of another prison for the imagination and the spiritual nature of man; this was complemented in the real world by the prison created by the iron laws of economics — the factory, the net of commerce and the house of industry are all aspects of it. In this bitter world of experience the child, symbol of human potentiality, languished. Similarly, Wordsworth saw his own generous aspirations defeated. Where now could one turn? At what point could the imagination re-enter and begin to change the world?

4 The Rainbow in the Mountains

22 J. M. W. Turner, Buttermere Lake, with Part of Cromackwater, Cumberland, a Shower (1798). Oil.

In this chapter we compare the discoveries made by landscape painters of the period with the new ideas about imagination which Wordsworth and Coleridge expounded in *Lyrical Ballads* (1798) and associated prose works (Wordsworth's *Preface* and Coleridge's *Biographia Literaria*). What is important is to realize that poets and artists were engaged in the exploration of truth in all its 'minute particulars', and that they were in no sense trying to romanticize what they saw. We may look back and see Turner's *Buttermere Lake* (22), with its visionary rainbow, as some kind

of equivalent to Wordsworth's Lake District scenes. Turner would, I think, have thought that he had done a good job in recording the weather. As he said in a lecture,

> What seems one day to be equally governed by one cause is destroyed the next by a different atmosphere. In our variable climate, where all the seasons are recognisable in one day, where all the vapoury turbulence involves the face of things, where nature seems to sport in all her dignity . . . how happily is the landscape painter situated, how roused by every change of nature in every moment, that allows of no langour, even in her effects, which she places before him, and demands most peremptorily every moment his admiration and investigation, to store his mind with every change of time and place.

This led painters to make several studies of the same scene under different atmospheric conditions, and to consider the changing effects of light. In this they were the true children of the eighteenth-century scientific revolution, however much we may regard them as Romantic artists.

Newton's Rainbow

The explanation of optical phenomena had been one of Newton's main areas of research. For this he was honoured by the poets of the eighteenth century; he had substituted truth for fiction, and there was no reason to regret such an advance. So James Thomson, in his verses *To the Memory of Sir Isaac Newton*, (1727), after listing his astronomical discoveries, continues

> Even Light itself, which every thing displays,
> Shone undiscovered, till his brighter mind
> Untwisted all the shining robe of day;
> And, from the whitening undistinguished blaze,
> Collecting every ray into his kind,
> To the charmed eye educed the gorgeous train
> Of parent colours. First the flaming red
> Sprung vivid forth; the tawny orange next;
> And next delicious yellow; by whose side
> Fell the kind beams of all-refreshing green.
> Then the pure blue, that swells autumnal skies,
> Ethereal played; and then, of sadder hue,
> Emerged the deepened indigo, as when
> The heavy-skirted evening droops with frost;
> While the last gleamings of refracted light
> Died in the fainting violet away.
> These, when the clouds distil the rosy shower,
> Shine out distinct adown the watery bow;
> While o'er our heads the dewy vision bends
> Delightful, melting on the fields beneath.
> Myriads of mingling dyes from these result,
> And myriads still remain—infinite source
> Of beauty, ever flushing, ever new.

Did ever poet image aught so fair,
Dreaming in whispering groves by the hoarse
    brook?
Or prophet, to whose rapture heaven descends?
Even now the setting sun and shifting clouds,
Seen, Greenwich, from thy lovely heights, declare
How just, how beauteous the refractive law.

(96-124)

In (23) Newton is seen at work with his prism; the painter had to go to a lot of trouble to get the spectrum the right way up. It is worth pointing out that though Blake rejected Newton for his 'single Vision', Wordsworth always refers to him in the most generous terms. This may be partly explained by his devotion to geometry as representing one kind of Truth; in the famous dream in *The Prelude*, (1805, Book V 64-5) 'Poetry and geometric Truth, the knowledge that endures,' are both given equal value.

23 George Romney, Newton and the Prism *(c.1794). Oil.*

Joseph Wright's landscape (24) shows a scene which we could presumably locate on the ground, if we lived near Chesterfield at the time. Into the sky rises the arch of the rainbow, depicted with the same kind of accurate observation. It has in fact been said that Wright is painting a scientific demonstration of a well-known natural phenomenon. The poetic equivalent might be this little effusion by Gilbert White of Selborne, the famous naturalist:

ON THE RAINBOW

'Look upon the Rainbow, and praise him that made it: very beautiful is it in the brightness thereof.' Eccles. xliii. 11.

On morning or on evening cloud impress'd,
Bent in vast curve, the wat'ry meteor shines
Delightfully, to th' levell'd sun oppos'd:
Lovely refraction! while the vivid brede
In listed colours glows, th' unconscious swain,
With vacant eye gazes on the divine
Phænomenon, gleaming o'er th' illumined fields,
Or runs to catch the treasures which it sheds.
 Not so the sage, inspir'd with pious awe;
He hails the federal arch; and looking up,
Adores that God, whose fingers form'd this bow
Magnificent, compassing heav'n about
With a resplendent verge. 'Thou mad'st the cloud,
'Maker omnipotent, and thou the bow;
'And by that covenant graciously hast sworn
'Never to drown the world again: henceforth,
'Till time shall be no more, in ceaseless round,
'Season shall follow season: day to night,
'Summer to winter, harvest to seed time,
'Heat shall to cold in regular array
'Succeed.'—Heav'n taught, so sang the Hebrew bard.

The first eight lines are to the point, but I print the poem in full to remind the reader of the Christian *meaning* of the rainbow as a symbol, to which Gilbert White, as a clergyman, might be expected to allude. This religious symbolism has, as it were, been banished by Newton's explanation. Is it in Joseph Wright's picture? I think not; but some critics have felt that Wright shows that there is something aery and insubstantial about the rainbow, so that it is not just an appearance, but in some sense a thing not of this world. It is a tribute to Joseph Wright's art that both interpretations have been offered; that is, that the rainbow is both a scientific and a visionary appearance, and that, such is the balance which the painting so delicately maintains, that both are simultaneously true. (Compare Joseph Wright's other work 29, 30 and 110.) I would contend that Wordsworth is trying in his natural descriptions — though is 'description' quite the right word? — to preserve the same balance as Wright, even though when the mists rise he is more akin to Turner. In both (22) and (24) the scene is in the real world, though our minds may invest it with poetic reality. We half-create the picture, as Wordsworth announced in the *Lines* known as *Tintern Abbey*,

> Therefore am I still
> A lover of the meadows and the woods,
> And mountains; and of all that we behold
> From this green earth; of all the mighty world
> Of eye, and ear — both what they half create,
> And what perceive. . .

The Moving Mountain

Let us take a specific example from Wordsworth's *Prelude* to illustrate this point. As a boy Wordsworth 'borrows' a boat one night and rows upon the lake:

> One evening (surely I was led by her)
> I went alone into a Shepherd's Boat,
> A Skiff that to a Willow tree was tied
> Within a rocky Cave, its usual home.
> 'Twas by the shores of Patterdale, a Vale
> Wherein I was a Stranger, thither come
> A School-boy Traveller, at the Holidays.
> Forth rambled from the Village Inn alone
> No sooner had I sight of this small Skiff,
> Discover'd thus by unexpected chance,
> Than I unloos'd her tether and embark'd.
> The moon was up, the Lake was shining clear
> Among the hoary mountains; from the Shore
> I push'd, and struck the oars and struck again
> In cadence, and my little Boat mov'd on

Even like a Man who walks with stately step
Though bent on speed. It was an act of stealth
And troubled pleasure; not without the voice
Of mountain-echoes did my Boat move on,
Leaving behind her still on either side
Small circles glittering idly in the moon,
Until they melted all into one track
Of sparkling light. A rocky Steep uprose
Above the Cavern of the Willow tree
And now, as suited one who proudly row'd
With his best skill, I fix'd a steady view
Upon the top of that same craggy ridge,
The bound of the horizon, for behind
Was nothing but the stars and the grey sky.
She was an elfin Pinnace; lustily
I dipp'd my oars into the silent Lake,
And, as I rose upon the stroke, my Boat
Went heaving through the water, like a Swan;
When from behind that craggy Steep, till then
The bound of the horizon, a huge Cliff,
As if with voluntary power instinct,
Uprear'd its head. I struck, and struck again,
And, growing still in stature, the huge Cliff
Rose up between me and the stars, and still,
With measur'd motion, like a living thing,
Strode after me. With trembling hands I turn'd,
And through the silent water stole my way
Back to the Cavern of the Willow tree.
There, in her mooring-place, I left my Bark,
And, through the meadows homeward went, with grave
And serious thoughts; and after I had seen
That spectacle, for many days, my brain
Work'd with a dim and undetermin'd sense
Of unknown modes of being; in my thoughts
There was a darkness, call it solitude,
Or blank desertion, no familiar shapes
Of hourly objects, images of trees,
Of sea or sky, no colours of green fields;
But huge and mighty Forms that do not live
Like living men mov'd slowly through the mind
By day and were the trouble of my dreams.

The Prelude, 1805 Book I, ll. 372–427

I have used the 1805 version of this incident rather than the more familiar 1850 text, because it establishes that the scene is Ullswater. Here are two photographs (25) which show how St Sunday's Crag appears to move behind and along the nearer hills at the lake's edge. It seems to me that the point of all this is to show that a 'real' event and an imaginative event have identical existence; this is the real strength of Wordsworth's imagination. It also turns the corner from the purely scientific perception of things which the Newtonian universe allowed; a way is found for the imagination to re-enter the familiar world of appearances. In this case the total perception has been 'half-created' by the imagination of a child.

25 *Two views of St Sunday's Crag from Ullswater.*

26 *Francis Danby*, Boys Sailing a
Little Boat *(c. 1821)*. *Watercolour*.

27 *Philipp Otto Runge*, The
Hülsenbeck Children *(1805-6)*. *Oil*.

The Child as Seer

Compare these two pictures. In the Danby painting (26) the children are seen by the adult mind engaged in a typically 'childish' activity; though there is sympathy they are seen from outside. (Nevertheless, to be fair to this very interesting picture, look at it again after reading the section on The Voyage of Life.) The Runge painting (27) is more difficult to understand; the children are wider-eyed than they should be, and there is something odd about the point of view, until we realise that this is a view from a child's eyes and at child eye-level. To Wordsworth, what the child saw was both more imaginative and more vivid than the casual perceptions of the adult; and the child's seeings, retained in the memory, provided food for future years of thought.

Wordsworth's Rainbow Poem

If we now put together everything we have so far looked at in this chapter we can move towards an appreciation of Wordsworth's Rainbow Poem:

> My heart leaps up when I behold
> A rainbow in the sky:
> So was it when my life began;
> So is it now I am a man;
> So be it when I shall grow old,
> Or let me die!
> The Child is father of the Man;
> And I could wish my days to be
> Bound each to each by natural piety.

Wordsworth recreates the message of the promise (in the Gilbert White poem) but in the terms of a new kind of faith. Here again, this is not the occasion for literary criticism, but an understanding of the Rainbow poem will lead to an appreciation of its fuller form in *Tintern Abbey*, and this in turn to the longer spelling out of the message in the *The Prelude*. Now look at the Friedrich picture (28). While there are references to reality in it the intention of the whole painting is symbolic. (Those not familiar with the work of this great German Romantic painter will find further examples at 32, 36, 39 and 83.) Notice the scale of the mountains and the rainbow in contrast with the tiny human figure below. The exact Christian symbolism which Friedrich read into his own paintings is not really necessary to our understanding; the suggestiveness is more in keeping with Romanticism. Friedrich is making a statement about human existence on earth and its limitations; the small figure (presumably the artist) sees consolation in the heavens. Although the landscape features stand for religious truths, there is a genuine feeling for the German landscape which parallels that of our own school of painters.

I would not myself agree with those who think that Friedrich 'illustrates' Wordsworth, though this painting is helpful in studying this one poem. In fact the symbolic world of Friedrich has closer affinities to the poetry of Coleridge; nevertheless the line from Joseph Wright to Turner to Friedrich is a good parallel to the general way in which Romantic poetry develops.

Effects of Light

Turner, it might be said, began by painting landscapes and ended painting light itself. Wordsworth and Coleridge constantly refer to effects of light when trying to illustrate the effects of the imagination. Consider this pair of pictures by Joseph Wright (29, 30), who was particularly fond of contrasts of this kind.* The scene is changed by the moonlight more than one might at first expect.

Wordsworth and his sister, Dorothy, together with Coleridge, often walked by moonlight when discussing the plans for the *Lyrical Ballads* in 1798. Coleridge says in *Biographia Literaria* that,

28 Caspar David Friedrich,
Mountain Landscape with
Rainbow *(c. 1810). Oil.*

29 Joseph Wright of Der
Dovedale in Sunlight
(c. 1784–88). Oil.

30 Joseph Wright of Der
Dovedale by Moonlight
(c. 1784–88). Oil.
Wordsworth visited
Dovedale on 8 June 1788

*For example *Arkwright's Cotton Mills by Day* and *by Night*—the latter showing an illuminated building indicating a night shift.

> . . . our conversations turned frequently on the two cardinal points of poetry, the power of exciting the sympathy of the reader by a faithful adherence to the truth of nature, and the power of giving the interest of novelty by the modifying colours of imagination. The sudden charm, which accidents of light and shade, which moonlight or sunset diffused over a known and familiar landscape, appeared to represent the practicability of combining both. These are the poetry of nature.

The many further references to moonlight in Wordsworth's poems, and to other kinds of light, would be a fruitful subject for further enquiry. The *Ode—Intimations of Immortality from Recollections of Early Childhood* looks back to a time when

> The earth, and every common sight,
> To me did seem
> Apparelled in celestial light . . .

but the very word 'Apparelled' implies the possibility of the withdrawal of that light.

From this point the argument of this chapter concerns itself exclusively with Coleridge (31), seen here as he would appear to the younger Romantics, shrouded in Gothic gloom. In the division of labour proposed at the time of composing the *Lyrical Ballads* Wordsworth was 'to give the charm of novelty to the things of every day' (as suggested above); Coleridge, on the other hand, was to direct his attention to 'persons and characters supernatural' to which he was to give 'human interest and a semblance of truth'. Before turning to *The Ancient Mariner*, which was Coleridge's principal contribution to the *Ballads*, I would like to continue to explore the effects of light which he frequently makes use of, to bring out the difference between the two poets.

Coleridge is fascinated by appearances of nature which are so unusual that they seem to be from another world. Here Friedrich (32) admirably illustrates one of these, the old moon in the new moon's arms, which is the subject of the first stanza of *Dejection: an Ode*. Friedrich's picture has been allegorized in the following way. Two figures, the one on the right Friedrich himself, look out from a stony path (the path of life); the dying oak tree and the dolmen to the right have pagan associations with death; the moon is a symbol of Christ, whose full shape, though not yet revealed, is seen in outline (the old moon). Though the allegory is for many people a limiting account of this uncanny painting, one notes that Coleridge, himself a Christian, said 'I had worshipped God in the moon' (*Notebooks* 2 March 1805). Further, on 14 April of the same year, he noted

> In looking at objects of Nature while I am thinking, as at yonder moon dim-glimmering through the dewy window-pane, I seem rather to be seeking, as it were *asking* for, a symbolical language for something within me that already and for ever exists, than observing anything new.

31 Washington Allston, S. T. Coleridge (1814). Oil. Shows Coleridge looking like a preacher; notice the Gothic window.

The Spectre and the Glory

32 Caspar David Friedrich,
Two Men Contemplating
the Moon *(1819). Oil.*

The final stage of this exploration of the effects of light is the transformation of the beholder, either into a menacing spirit or into a saint. A man sees himself projected on to a cloud, and, as Coleridge notes: 'The beholder either recognizes it as a projected form of his own being, that moves before him with a glory round its head, or recoils from it as a spectre.' Coleridge visited the Hartz mountains, and made unsuccessful attempts to see the Brocken spectre (33) on two occasions, and alludes to it in the poem *Constancy to an Ideal Object*. Coleridge's notebooks are full of similar observations of strange phenomena, such as moon-rainbows (22 October 1801). The poetic *use* he makes of them is to illustrate mental states; but to do this the poetic material must be fully absorbed and digested by the imagination.

33a Modern photograph showing the image of the observer projected onto the cloud. The head is surrounded by a ring of light.

33b The Glory seen by John Haygarth near the Vale of Clwyd, *from John Haygarth's article in* Memoirs of the Literary and Philosophical Society of Manchester *(1790) Vol. 3 pp. 463–7. Frequently referred to by Coleridge, e.g. 'an image with a glory round its head' occurs in* Constancy to an Ideal Object. *For the frightening aspects see the* Doppelgänger *(113).*

Fancy and Imagination

Consider these two architectural fantasies: in Marlow's *Capriccio* (34) a scene by a Venetian Canal is deliberately and carefully juxtaposed with St Paul's, London; in Gandy's watercolour (35) we are meant to note the care with which the artist has reproduced 'Architecture from the school of Constantinople of the 6th and 7th centuries' though in fact the Byzantine references are hardly the most prominent. I think Coleridge would have seen in the Marlow the exercise of the faculty which he called *fancy*, which deals with 'fixities and definites. The fancy is no other than a mode of memory emancipated from the order of time and space.' In the Gandy, on the other hand, memories of Roslin Chapel blend in with whatever he had been able to learn of the Byzantines, so that the picture illustrates Coleridge's Imagination, which 'dissolves, diffuses, dissipates, in order to re-create.' Gandy was also trying to illustrate a passage from Harrington's translation of Ariosto:

> This was a church most solemn and devout
> And rais'd by art on arches all about
> And straight she saw the stately tomb erected
> Of marble pure. . . .
> The very marble was so clear and bright
> That though the sun no light into it gave
> The Tomb itself did lighten all the cave.

As Sir John Summerson has pointed out* it is the reversal of normal lighting which makes this picture so uncanny. He compares the lighting of *Christabel*, and sees this as a visual analogue of that poem, as well as of the 'intricate archaeological romance of Sir Walter Scott'. One notes, with regard to the theme of this chapter, that which started as an investigation of the light of nature has concluded in a vision of the light of the imagination, pouring out from somewhere deep within the cavern of the subconscious mind.

*Sir John Summerson, *Heavenly Mansions*, New York, 1963, pp. 128–30.

34 *William Marlow,*
Capriccio: St Paul's and a
Venetian Canal *(c. 1795).*
Oil. The juxtaposition of
two scenes to produce either
an effect of dissonance
(Past against Present), or
to link two commercial
capitals of great empires.

35 *Joseph Michael Gandy,*
The Tomb of Merlin
(1815). Watercolour.
Gandy is sometimes
described as the English
Piranesi: see (66), (67)
and (112).

5 The Voyage of Life

In this chapter we are primarily concerned with pictures which illuminate the understanding of the various levels of meaning in *The Ancient Mariner*; but the chain of imagery connecting life and water-borne travellers will lead us to further consideration of Wordsworth, and allow us to look forward to the work of Shelley.

Coleridge tells us that at least one of the sources of *The Ancient Mariner* was a friend's dream. Though the poem has always made good sense when read purely at the literal level, it draws upon such an enormous stock of imagery that religious and psychological interpretations have become commonplace. One of Friedrich's more mysterious pictures, *The Stages of Life* (36), is similarly valid on two levels, both as a study of twilight on the Baltic Sea, and as an allegory of human life. The subject-matter, too, provides a possible way into Coleridge's poem.

In *The Stages of Life* the five looming ships have been linked with the five figures in the foreground. The old man with a stick, his back turned towards us, is thought to be Friedrich himself: as he approaches the shore, the largest vessel comes towards him. To the right are his wife and children, separated from him by the beckoning man. The two little children are matched by the two boats setting out from the shore; presumably the two figures in middle life relate to the two ships on the horizon, far out yet beginning to return. The beckoning man is the hardest figure to interpret; he seems to be telling Friedrich something about the children, who are absorbed in raising a tiny Swedish flag. (This again seems to have some meaning; there is a passage in Kafka's *The Castle* where the planting of a tiny flag upon a wall is an affirmation of life.) The sunset is associated with death; there is a tiny crescent moon to the left of the large ship, just above the cloudbank. In Friedrich's symbolism, as we have already seen, this represents salvation through Christ. This would seem to confirm that the ships are not in any sense menacing, though their inexorable movement indicates a fatalistic view of life. There are many other paintings by Friedrich of ships and the seashore which help to confirm these interpretations.

36 *Caspar David Friedrich*, The Stages of Life *(c. 1835). Oil.*

Exploration

As is well known, *The Ancient Mariner* is, even on the literal level, a poem of the imagination, for at the time of writing Coleridge had never been to sea. Coleridge and Wordsworth were great readers of travel books, partly, it must be admitted, for the stores of imagery which they contained; but remember that so much of the earth's surface was still unexplored that a taste for reading about voyages of discovery was no less contemporary in 1798 than the modern interest in space-travel. *The Ancient Mariner* is a distant cousin of science fiction.

The map (37) is taken from a geography textbook for children — *The Young Lady's and Gentleman's Atlas for Assisting them in the Knowledge of Geography* — published in 1805 and reprinted in 1822, so that it was in use

37 *Map of the world—from John Adams*, The Young Lady's and Gentleman's Atlas for Assisting them in the Knowledge of Geography *(1805, reprinted 1822).*

for most of our period of study. Many better and more elaborate atlases existed, of course, but I wanted to show the general rather than the geographer's picture of the world. While not pretending that this is a very careful production, I think that some of the detail is fascinating; Turkey, for example, is spread between Europe and Asia. Much of the earth's land surface was still unexplored by Europeans, though advances were being made in America, Asia and Australia; the interior of Africa was quite unknown.

The sea, on the other hand, was now navigable up to the great ice barrier, thanks to advances in technology and scientific instruments. The tracks on the map are those of Captain Cook; note especially the Southern Icy Ocean and the absence of the Antarctic continent. This illustration to Cook's *Voyages* (38) gives us the literal equivalent of

> The ice was here, the ice was there

besides giving a kind of poetic grandeur to the scene. It is also possible that Coleridge obtained information about the Southern Ocean from William Wales, the astronomer of the first voyage of the *Resolution*; he became mathematics master at Christ's Hospital, where Coleridge was at school.

38 J. Webber, Resolution in the Ice with Discovery *(1809). Coloured aquatint.*

The Sea of Ice

On a symbolic level Friedrich (39) again helps us to see the deeper
meaning. The sea of ice is a sea of death; *The Hope* (symbolic name) is
seen to the right, small in size, crushed and utterly destroyed by the
immense forces of an alien world. In this bleak landscape there is no
indication of any future redemption. Coleridge, of course, introduces the
Albatross.

The Albatross

Traditionally, the albatross was always regarded as the bringer of wind
and fog. The Wandering Albatross is the largest of these birds, with an
eleven-foot wing-span; it needs the wind in order to fly. Coleridge is also
right in stating that the mariners fed the albatross, since these birds do
not fear man. That to kill them is to invite bad luck is also a traditional
belief. Wordsworth suggested the shooting to Coleridge; he had been
reading in Shelvocke's *Voyage to the Southern Ocean* of how 'Captain
Hartley shot an Albatross'.

The range of reference which the Albatross suggests can be exaggerated. It is surely not to be taken as Christ, though the poem does suggest a religious dimension—the bird is hailed as 'a Christian soul', and it perches 'for vespers nine'. In discussing the poem Professor J. Livingstone Lowes* pointed to an interesting parallel in Herman Melville's notes to *Moby Dick*:

> I remember the first albatross I ever saw. It was during a prolonged gale, in waters hard upon the Antarctic seas. From my forenoon watch below, I ascended to the overclouded deck; and there, dashed upon the main hatches, I saw a regal, feathery thing of unspotted whiteness, and with a hooked, Roman bill sublime. At intervals, it arched forth its vast archangel wings, as if to embrace some holy ark. Wonderous flutterings and throbbings shook it. Though bodily unharmed, it uttered cries, as some king's ghost in supernatural distress. Through its inexpressible, strange eyes, methought I peeped to secrets which took hold of God. As Abraham before the angels, I bowed myself; the white thing was so white, its wings so wide, and in those for ever exiled waters, I had lost the miserable warping memories of traditions and of towns. Long I gazed at that prodigy of plumage. I cannot tell, can only hint, the things that darted through me then. . . . By no possibility could Coleridge's wild Rhyme have had aught to do with those mystical impressions that were mine, when I saw that bird upon our deck. For neither had I then read the Rhyme, nor knew the bird to be an albatross. Yet, in saying this, I do but indirectly burnish a little brighter the noble merit of the poem and the poet.

The illustration (40) is from a complete series by Gustave Doré. Although he was not a contemporary of the Romantics, and was therefore at times liable to look for the horrible or the pious scenes in what is already a very melodramatic vision of the universe, his style does seem to fit this poem. In addition, the particular details of his illustrations show a deep reading of the poem, and his occasional supplying of extra material usually serves to bring out Coleridge's meaning.**

Cain

For his crime the Mariner undergoes a severe penance; some feel this is out of all proportion to the crime. It is of course true that Coleridge and Wordsworth were originally trying to write a ballad about 'The Wanderings of Cain'; Wordsworth felt unable to collaborate in this, and 'the Ancient Mariner was written instead'. The Mariner differs from Cain in that he is ignorant, and shoots without realizing that the bird is protected by a spirit; on the other hand the machinery of the poem reinforces the 'moral', in which we are taught that all things 'man, and bird and beast' are equally loved by God. In this sense the Albatross is a brother. The Cain theme must therefore be considered seriously for a moment to establish its relevance to the imagery.

40 *Gustave Doré,* Shoo the Albatross, *from Samuel Taylor Coleridg* The Rime of the Ancie Mariner, *illustrated by Gustave Doré (1875). Wood engraving.*

*in *The Road to Xanadu.* (Constable, 1927).
**Reprinted as *The Rime of the Ancient Mariner* with 42 illustrations by Gustave Doré (Dover Publications, 1970).

41 *William Blake*, The Body of Abel found by Adam and Eve *(c. 1826)*. *Pen and tempera, in places over gold, on mahogany. In 1822 Blake wrote* The Ghost of Abel, *a short drama on the same subject, which is dedicated to 'Lord Byron in the Wilderness'.*

Blake (41) conveys the horror of the Bible story—look at the figure of Adam to the right, and the strange oval shape formed by Eve's arms. The sun is darkened and Cain is pursued by what look like furious vibrations or tongues of fire. Notice how he clutches his brow. In *Genesis* his punishment is to 'be a fugitive and a vagabond in the earth', and he carries a mark (traditionally on his brow) 'lest any finding him should kill him'. In the Mariner's case, he too will be given a punishment worse than the death allowed to the rest of the crew, and this will compel him to wander continually; as a mark of his crime the Albatross is hung about his neck.

The Water Snakes

This illustration (42) shows the Mariner alone. In his dejection he seems beyond hope of redemption. But two things happen: the moon rises into the sky (not shown in the illustration, but notice the cross-reference to the moon-symbol in Friedrich), and the Mariner inadvertently blesses the water snakes; Doré's beasts are rather larger than one might expect.

> The moving Moon went up the sky,
>   And no where did abide:
> Softly she was going up,
>   And a star or two beside . . .
>
> Beyond the shadow of the ship,
>   I watched the water-snakes:
> They moved in tracks of shining white,
> And when they reared, the elfish light
>   Fell off in hoary flakes.

42 *Gustave Doré* The
Watersnakes, *see (40)*.

Within the shadow of the ship
   I watched their rich attire:
Blue, glossy green, and velvet black,
They coiled and swam; and every track
   Was a flash of golden fire.

O happy living things! no tongue
   Their beauty might declare:
A spring of love gushed from my heart,
   And I blessed them unaware:
Sure my kind saint took pity on me,
   And I blessed them unaware.

The self-same moment I could pray;
   And from my neck so free
The Albatross fell off, and sank
   Like lead into the sea.

Part IV 283–6 and 272–91

I have quoted these lines in full as they are the heart of the poem. Notice that the psychological story is the same as that told in *The Prelude* and other Wordsworth poems—Despondency is corrected, and Imagination restored—and resembles that in Chapter V of John Stuart Mill's *Autobiography* ('A Crisis in my Mental History'), where a chance release from an obsessive melancholy state was provided by 'the culture of the feelings' found in the poetry of Wordsworth. Think how in *Tintern Abbey* the forms of Nature

> . . . have no slight or trivial influence
> On that best portion of a good man's life,
> His little, nameless, unremembered, acts
> Of kindness and of love.

It has been suggested that all these 'stories', though no longer explicitly Christian, derive from Wesley's preaching: the soul must undergo conversion, and be born again. From this point Coleridge's poem moves towards salvation; the return home is particularly well illustrated by Doré. It seems to me that the sinking of the vessel as it enters the mouth of the harbour is yet another link to Friedrich's *The Stages of Life* (36).

The Wanderer

This is the last Doré illustration (43). The Wedding-Guest, suitably chastened, has 'turned from the Bridegroom's door'. The Mariner is destined to continue his wanderings. Such a strange Wanderer will recur again and again in Romantic literature. Consider, for example, Wordsworth's Pedlars, and other solitary figures such as the Leech Gatherer. In Byron's work the exile is usually the hero, and he often bears a mark like Cain's. (From Cain there is a numerous progeny in Byron's heroic figures, and there is a further link to the Prometheus-Satan theme.) Indeed, some of the Romantic poets may be said to imitate art in their lives; Wordsworth said that his hobby was wandering, and De Quincey calculated that he must have *walked* between 175,000 and 180,000 miles in his lifetime; Shelley and Byron, too, however necessary their exile, seem to live out this great Romantic image, whose origins are far earlier than the Romantic period.

In the Middle Ages a story circulated concerning the Wandering Jew, an old man who moved restlessly about Europe looking for death; it is possible that this is an allegorical representation of the exile and persecution of the Jewish nation. Shelley retells the story in the *Notes to Queen Mab*, (VII, l.67) saying that what follows is 'a translation of part of some German work, whose title I have vainly endeavoured to discover. I picked it up, dirty and torn, some years ago, in Lincoln's Inn Fields'.

43 Gustave Doré, The
Ancient Mariner leaves
the Wedding Guest and
continues his Wandering
*see (40). Doré transposes
the scene to a medieval
French setting when land is
reached.*

When our Lord was wearied with the burthen of His ponderous cross, and wanted
to rest before the door of Ahasuerus, the unfeeling wretch drove him away with
brutality. The Saviour of mankind staggered, sinking under the heavy load, but
uttered no complaint. An angel of death appeared before Ahasuerus, and
exclaimed indignantly, 'Barbarian! thou has denied rest to the Son of Man; be it
denied thee also, until He comes to judge the world.'

So this suffering, tired, guilt-laden figure, goaded on by an avenging
deity, travels from land to land. As a result of his wanderings, the original
crime is expiated, and a further development of the character results. The
Wanderer, because of his accumulated historical experience, acquires
secret Knowledge: again notice the link to the Prometheus story. This

Knowledge may be geographical (location of secret passages, gold), occult (magic, power to summon spirits), moral (as in *The Ancient Mariner*), or prophetic (future of individuals, nations, the world). The course of this development of the original story can be traced throughout Shelley's poetry, starting with *Ghasta, or the Avenging Demon!!!* and ending with *Hellas*, where Ahasuerus is summoned from his cave to prophesy the future of the Turkish Empire.

The final stage is the realization that all these wanderings take place in the world of the imagination; the poet himself is the wanderer, exploring the secret places of the mind, which is itself a labyrinth. (See front endpaper and p. 149.) In her note on *Prometheus Unbound* Mary Shelley quotes a comment written by Shelley on Sophocles' *Oedipus Tyrannus*, line 67, which I cite in full because of its general relevance to the understanding of Romantic imagery:

> In the Greek Shakespeare, Sophocles, we find the image,
>
> Πολλὰς δ'ὸδοὺς ἐλθόντα φροντίδος πλάνοις:
>
> a line of almost unfathomable depth of poetry; yet how simple are the images in which it is arrayed!
>
>   'Coming to many ways in the wanderings of careful thought.'
>
> If the words ὸδοὺς and πλάνοις had not been used, the line might have been explained in a metaphorical instead of an absolute sense, as we say '*ways* and means,' and 'wanderings' for error and confusion. But they meant literally paths or roads, such as we tread with our feet; and wanderings, such as a man makes when he loses himself in a desert, or roams from city to city—as Oedipus, the speaker of this verse, was destined to wander, blind and asking charity. What a picture does this line suggest of the mind as a wilderness of intricate paths, wide as the universe, which is here made its symbol; a world within a world which he who seeks some knowledge with respect to what he ought to do searches throughout, as he would search the external universe for some valued thing which was hidden from him upon its surface.

The archetypal figure of Oedipus opens up further vistas into the classical hinterland—Ulysses, Aeneas—as well as psychological depths which I do not intend to pursue. For there is one more chain of imagery in Coleridge and Wordsworth which will help us to complete the synthesizing work of this chapter.

The River

Let us return to the 'spring of love' which gushed from the heart of the Mariner. Further on, in one of the stanzas of the fifth section of the poem, there occurs this image:

> A noise like of a hidden brook
> In the leafy month of June
> That to the sleeping woods all night
> Singeth a quiet tune.

While existing in its own right, there may be a link from this simile to another project of the *Lyrical Ballads* period.

While working together in 1797–8 Wordsworth and Coleridge thought of writing a poem called *The Brook*, in which the course of a river would be traced from source to mouth. Now there are two passages at least in *The Prelude* where comparisons are made between the course of a river and the pattern of an individual's life. In one (1850, Book IV, ll. 256 ff) the poet contemplating his past life is compared to

> . . . one who hangs down-bending from the side
> Of a slow-moving boat, upon the breast
> Of a still water . . .

The whole passage is too complicated in its reference to be considered in full at this juncture, but should be looked at. The second (1850, Book XIV, ll. 193–205) is more relevant to the simple comparison; a river is used to show how in tracing his life Wordsworth has always been conscious of the Faculty of Imagination:

> This faculty hath been the feeding source
> Of our long labour: we have traced the stream
> From the blind cavern whence is faintly heard
> Its natal murmur; followed it to light
> And open day; accompanied its course
> Among the ways of Nature, for a time
> Lost sight of it bewildered and engulphed;
> Then given it greeting as it rose once more
> In strength, reflecting from its placid breast
> The works of man and face of human life;
> And lastly, from its progress have we drawn
> Faith in life endless, the sustaining thought
> Of human Being, Eternity, and God.

Notice here first 'the blind cavern' which we will try to explore later (p. 67); secondly 'rose once more'—the rebirth theme already mentioned; and finally the presumed meeting with the sea of eternity, though this is not clearly seen here. In fact, Wordsworth made the course of a river the subject of an exceptionally good sonnet-sequence, *The River Duddon*, and in Sonnet XXXIII 'The Wanderer' and 'thy Poet, cloud-born stream' are

> Prepared, in peace of heart, in calm of mind
> And soul, to mingle with Eternity!

as the river meets the sea.

44 *Edward Dayes*,
Tintern Abbey *(1794)*.
Watercolour.

Edward Dayes' picture (44), with its generous sweep of river and trees, is an appropriate illustration to the poem usually known as *Tintern Abbey*; after all, the poet is less concerned with that religious foundation than he is with 'Revisiting the Banks of the Wye.' The major theme of the poem is the restorative power of memory, particularly the memory of natural objects, and I have alluded to these matters, however briefly, in discussing the Rainbow poem. The point I would like to make here, which I think is helpful to a reader coming to this very complicated poem for the first time, is that one should notice the references to the river in *Tintern Abbey*, including the more subtle verbal associations in key-words like 'rolls' and 'impels'. Even 'felt along the heart' makes sense in this context. We are repeatedly informed that we are standing on the banks of a stream, which seems to be symbolically related to human life —

> How oft in spirit have I turned to thee
> O Sylvan Wye! thou *wanderer* through the woods . . . (my italics)

At this point the whole pattern is complete.

The Voyage of Life

It was given to the Victorians to spell out what the Romantics saw in glimpses: Tennyson's *The Brook* is a late rendering of the poem Wordsworth and Coleridge never had time to write. In any case, one must not exaggerate the gap between the Romantic and the Victorian periods which is much narrower than we often want to realize. Byron,

Shelley and Keats, if they had lived, would have been the great Victorian poets, perhaps surviving into the 1880s. Thomas Cole, the American painter of the Hudson River School, began in 1839 to paint a series of pictures entitled *The Voyage of Life* (45 i, ii, iii & iv).

I print Cole's own commentary on the series; look in the pictures for the synthesis of all the imagery we have been discussing: the Wanderer makes his Voyage along the Stream of Life.

1. CHILDHOOD. —A stream is seen issuing from a deep cavern, in the side of a craggy and precipitous mountain, whose summit is den in clouds. From out the cave glides a Boat, whose golden prow and sides are sculptured into figures of the Hours. Steered by Angelic Form, and laden with buds and flowers, it bears a laughing Infant, the Voyager, whose varied course the Artist has empted to delineate. On either hand, the banks of the stream are clothed in luxuriant herbage and flowers. The rising sun bathes mountains and flowery banks with rosy light.

The dark cavern is emblematic of our earthly origin, and the mysterious Past. The Boat, composed of figures of the Hours, images thought, that we are borne on the hours down the Stream of Life. The Boat identifies the subject in each picture. The rosy light of morning, the luxuriant flowers and plants, are emblems of the joyousness of early life. The close banks, and the limited scope of scene, indicates the narrow experience of Childhood, and the nature of its pleasures and desires. The Egyptian Lotus, in the eground of the picture, is symbolical of human Life. Joyousness and wonder are the characteristic emotions of childhood.

67

2. YOUTH.—The stream now pursues its course through a landscape of wider scope, and more diversified beauty. Trees of rich growth overshadow its banks, and verdant hills form the base of lofty mountains. The Infant of the former scene is become a Youth, on the verge of Manhood. He is now alone in the Boat, and takes the helm himself, and, in an attitude of confidence and eager expectation, gazes on a cloudy pile of Architecture, an air-built Castle, that rises dome above dome in the far-off blue sky. The Guardian Spirit stands upon the bank of the stream, and, with serious, yet benignant countenance, seems to be bidding the impetuous Voyager God speed. The beautiful stream flows for a distance, directly toward the aerial palace; but at length makes a sudden turn, and is seen in glimpses beneath the trees, until it at last descends with rapid current into a rocky ravine, where the Voyager will be found in the next picture. Over the remote hills, which seem to intercept the stream, and turn in from its hitherto direct course, a path is dimly seen, tending directly toward that cloudy Fabric, which is the object and desire of the Voyager.

The scenery of the picture—its clear stream, its lofty trees, its towering mountains, its unbounded distance, and transparent atmosphere—figure forth the romantic beauty of youthful imaginings, when the mind elevates the mean and Common into the Magnificent, before experience teaches what is the Real. The gorgeous cloud-built palace, whose glorious domes seem yet but half revealed to the eye, growing more and more lofty as we gaze, is emblematic of the daydreams of youth, its aspirations after glory and fame; and the dimly-seen path would intimate that Youth, in its impetuous career, is forgetful that it is embarked on the Stream of Life, and that its current sweeps along with resistless force, and increases in swiftness, as it descends toward the great ocean of Eternity.

3. MANHOOD. — Storm and cloud enshroud a rugged and dreary landscape. Bare, impending precipices rise in the lurid light. The swollen stream rushes furiously down a dark ravine, whirling and foaming in its wild career, and speeding toward the Ocean, which is dimly seen through the mist and falling rain. The boat is there plunging amid the turbulent waters. The Voyager is now a man of middle age: the helm of the boat is gone, and he looks imploringly towards heaven, as if heaven's aid alone could save him from the perils that surround him. The Guardian Spirit calmly sits in the clouds, watching, with an air of solicitude, the affrighted Voyager: Demon forms are hovering in the air.

Trouble is characteristic of the period of Manhood. In childhood, there is no carking care: in youth, no despairing thought. It is only when experience has taught us the realities of the world, that we lift from our eyes the golden veil of early life; that we feel deep and abiding sorrow: and in the Picture, the gloomy, eclipse-like tone, the conflicting elements, the trees riven by tempest, are the allegory; and the Ocean, dimly seen, figures the end of life, which the Voyager is now approaching. The demon forms are Suicide, Intemperance and Murder; which are the temptations that beset men in their direst trouble. The upward and imploring look of the Voyager shows his dependence on a Superior Power; and *that* faith saves him from the destruction that seems inevitable.

4. OLD AGE.—Portentous clouds are brooding over a vast and midnight Ocean. A few barren rocks are seen through the gloom—the last shores of the world. These form the mouth of the river; and the Boat, shattered by storms, its figures of the Hours broken and drooping, is seen gliding over the deep waters. Directed by the Guardian Spirit, who thus far has accompanied him *unseen*, the Voyager, now an old man, looks upward to an opening in the clouds, from whence a glorious light bursts forth; and angels are seen descending the cloudy steps, as if to welcome him to the Haven of Immortal Life.

The stream of life has now reached the Ocean to which all life is tending. The world to Old Age is destitute of interest. There is no longer any green thing upon it. The broken and drooping figures of the Boat show that time is nearly ended. The chains of corporeal existence are falling away; and already the mind has glimpses of Immortal Life. The angelic Being, of whose presence, until now, the Voyager has been unconscious, is revealed to him; and, with a countenance beaming with joy, shows to his wondering gaze scenes such as the eye of mortal man has never beheld.

After all this, my comments may seem superfluous. Much of the imagery here is common to Romantic poetry as a whole, and there is not space even to begin to follow up all the cross-references which this series of paintings brings to mind. Two examples from Coleridge's work must suffice. In *Kubla Khan*, Alph, the sacred river, rises from a chasm, meanders with a mazy motion, and finally sinks 'in tumult to a lifeless ocean'; this course corresponds roughly to the four pictures in the series. As I intend to explore aspects of this important poem later, this is simply a signpost at this point. Now look carefully at the last picture in the series, with its obvious *Ancient Mariner* links; if we delete the angel and the religious message (which seems in a way to confirm my impression that Cole the commentator didn't really know what Cole the painter was doing), consider how well it illustrates these lines from *Constancy to An Ideal Object*, where Coleridge again uses an image of utter desolation:

> . . . a becalméd bark,
> Whose Helmsman on an ocean waste and wide
> Sits mute and pale his mouldering helm beside.

Considered as a whole, Thomas Cole's series best illustrates Shelley's *Alastor*, in which the wanderings of the young poet along streams and rivers—or upon the ocean in the most unseaworthy little boat—make reference to all the symbolic associations we have now accumulated. The second generation of Romantic poets will, as a matter of course, have access to the imagery which the first generation laboured to create, and will be able to use it almost as a kind of shorthand. Shelley, as has often been observed, is continually fascinated by the lure of boats and the sea, but we should now be able to appreciate that

> . . . my spirit's bark is driven,
> Far from the shore, far from the trembling throng
> Whose sails were never to the tempest given
>
> *Adonais*

is not a prophecy of his own death so much as yet another recapitulation of the imagery depicted here.

6 Napoleon

In this section we look at the figure or image projected by Napoleon, and at the reactions of English poets to his rise and fall; we are not concerned with trying to establish the historical truth about the man himself. It is not necessary to relate Napoleon's conquests and achievements in detail, because this information is easily available; on the other hand, it will be necessary to focus sharply on one or two incidents.

The Image of Napoleon

In the British version of history Napoleon has always had a bad press. It is difficult for us to see that to the liberals of certain countries (e.g. Italy) he must have appeared as an apostle of the Revolution and a liberator of enslaved peoples, or to understand the feelings cherished by writers like Stendhal in the period of reaction after 1815.

David (46) shows the young general following in the footsteps of Hannibal and other great heroes. There are many similar French paintings, as we might expect; two good examples are *Bonaparte at Arcoli* by Gros, and *The Triumph of Bonaparte* by Prud'hon. All these could simply be dismissed as propaganda; even if we are generously inclined, there remains something ridiculous about the theatricality of the poses which are often copied from Michelangelo. In addition, since we do not go in for the renaming of streets which seems to characterize 'continental' dictatorships, it is utterly repugnant to us to learn that the constellation of Orion was renamed 'Napoleon'; and the remoulding of Europe, a truly Promethean task by any standards, is best summarized for us in the political cartoons of Gillray and others (47); the breaking down of the old order, and the setting up of new kingdoms and republics (equally fragile) takes place in a squalid kitchen; old Boney is up to his tricks again.

46 Jacques Louis David Bonaparte Crossing the Alps *(1800). Oil. Notic the names on the stones a bottom left.*

Invasion Scares

It is the threat of invasion which unites the nation; French conquests in Europe, notably the subjugation of Switzerland, had completed the disillusionment of many English Liberals like Wordsworth, who had originally been sympathetic to the French Revolution. Coleridge's *Fears in Solitude*, written in April 1798, shows one reaction. From 1802 Wordsworth produced his Sonnets dedicated to Liberty, such as 'Milton, thou shouldst be living at this hour'; he was later actively engaged in the formation of a volunteer force to resist the French.

The greatest scare lasted from May 1803 to July 1805; 'the Army of England' was encamped at Boulogne, with 2,000 vessels or landing-craft at their disposal; they were supposedly capable of deploying secret weapons, and attacking by air and underground as well as by sea (48). In fact, the sea-route was the *only* possible means of assault, and this was effectively blocked by the British Fleet. Napoleon made threats and loud noises which impressed nobody while the Channel remained secure; his nautical genius was seen by Gillray through the eyes of Dean Swift (49), and reminds us how well grounded in the eighteenth-century classics the reading public must have been. Gulliver is showing off at the court of Brobdingnag and thinks himself such a fine fellow; the giants, remarkable for their gentleness and large-mindedness, tolerate his antics, though they could have obliterated him in an instant. The cartoon is also remarkable for its portraiture of the King and Queen; it catches just the atmosphere of George III's court.

47 *James Gillray*, Tiddy-Doll, the great French-Gingerbread-Baker; drawing out a new batch of Kings—his Man, Hopping Talley, mixing up the Dough. *Published 23 January 1806. Engraving.* 'Tiddy-Doll', *who died in 1752, was a well-known streetseller of gingerbread cakes.*

48 Projects for a Frenc[h] Invasion of England. *Anonymous engraving. (c. 1805).*

49 *James Gillray*, The King of Brobdingnag a[nd] Gulliver. *Published 10 February 1804. Engravi[ng] after an original watercolour by Lt-Col. Braddyll. Scene:* 'Gulli[ver] manoeuvring his little bo[at] in the Cistern'.

The Peninsula

After 1805 (Battle of Trafalgar) the fear of invasion receded, and later the British began, in a small way, to venture forces in the Iberian Peninsula. In 1808 the Spanish people rose in revolt against the French; Goya's picture (50) is pivotal; after this the Romantic case against Napoleon was clear. As Wordsworth said: 'from the moment of the rising of the people of the Pyrenean peninsula, there was a mighty change'. The French, so-called promulgators of liberty, are here suppressing the national aspirations and the independence of the Spanish people. Goya's picture shows the reprisals which took place after the rising of 2 May; it is not necessary to assume that those being executed had any part in the rising: they may be quite innocent. The firing-squad, faceless, performs its task with brutal regularity. Those already shot are lying on the ground to the left of the picture; those being executed are standing behind the corpses; and further groups of four or five are queueing up, the leading figure having his hands over his face. The man in the white shirt is depicted standing in the attitude of the Crucifixion; there is a hole in the palm of his right hand. The dimly seen figure to the extreme left of the painting looks like an old woman with a child in her arms, and is possibly a reference to the Virgin Mary. Similarly, the Church in the background may have a symbolic reference.*

50 Goya, The Third of May, 1808: Execution of Rebels *(1814)*. Oil. *The executions took place at the Montaña del Príncipe Pío, Madrid—the hill in the background to the left. The buildings may simply represent the view from this spot at the time.*

*Though exactly what is difficult to decide. See Hugh Thomas, *The Third of May 1808* (Art in Context series, Allen Lane the Penguin Press) for further discussion of the points raised here.

From this time Wordsworth felt that to combat Napoleon was to be 'in sympathy with the species'; it ceased to matter that the French had originally stood for more liberal ideas than the mixture of religious fanaticism and blind nationalism for which the man in the white shirt may be dying.

As a result of the Spanish rising large areas of the country were temporarily free of French domination; *guerillas* (a new word dating from this war) operated behind the French lines. It was therefore a reasonable assumption to suppose that the British troops in Portugal would take a full part in the struggle, and Wordsworth and many others now concerned with pushing the war forward to a bloody conclusion were amazed to hear that the British generals had signed the Convention of Cintra by which the French were not only allowed to retreat unharmed but were actually given British transport to assist them. Wordsworth was moved to produce a political pamphlet, the *Tract on the Convention of Cintra*, from which the two quotations above have been taken. In fact, Wordsworth was now a supporter of any government which would prosecute a vigorous war-policy against 'the Despot', as Napoleon now appeared to him to be. He thus arrived at the right-wing political position which so shocked the younger Romantics.

Napoleon Falls

In this German caricature (51) the various stages of Napoleon's career are traced. At the bottom of the picture he is offered the island of Elba. One

The Rise and Fall of
..poleon *(1814)*.
..onymous caricature.
..ter climbing to the height
..being emperor (Kaiser*)*
..descends via Spain,
..oscow and Germany.
..nally he is offered the
..le island of Elba
..nderneath). Could also
..considered as a graph of
..stature among European
..erals.

wonders what ordinary people in England actually felt about Napoleon, and in particular what would have been the reaction of 'educated working men'. In Cobbett's *Political Register*, which would have been widely read by those of any Radical or Reformist sympathies, we read that his mistake had been to ally himself with 'the old Royal race' of Europe, who have now turned against him.

> He had the power of doing great good; he had the power to give freedom to all Europe; he did much good to France; he established, or rather, he did not destroy, the good laws which the Republicans had made; he did not bring back and replant the curses, which the Republicans had rooted out: France, under him, was much happier than France before the revolution. But, the lovers of freedom put great means into his hands; he had a mind calculated to give effect to those means; he did, for a while, employ them well; but being seized with the vanity of being a king, and with that most abominable itch of being a *papa* and leaving a son, descended from a mother of the old Royal race, he, from that moment, wholly abandoned the good cause, and laid the foundations of what has now come to pass.

Restoration of the Bourbons

The situation of the new generation of Romantic poets, Shelley, Byron and Keats, which may temporarily be summarized as 'political alienation,' stems from the settlement made at the Congress of Vienna. The decision was made to collaborate in an act of collective amnesia; the French Revolution, Napoleon, liberal ideas, the claims of the people, in short most things that had happened since 1789—all these were to be set aside and forgotten. Legitimacy was restored to France in the person of Louis XVIII, seen here in front of the throne of his fathers (52). On hearing the news, Byron, who had been keeping a journal, gave up in disgust:

> And all our *yesterdays* have lighted fools
> The way to dusty death.
> I will keep no further journal of that same hesternal torchlight: and, to prevent me from returning, like a dog, to the vomit of memory, I tear out the remaining leaves of this volume, and write, in *Ipecacuanha*—'that the Bourbons are restored!!!'— 'Hang up philosophy.' To be sure, I have long despised myself and man, but I never spat in the face of my species before—'O fool! I shall go mad.'

Here, in a picture whose horror still assaults the senses, is the kind of imagery which fits Byron's mood. Goya shows how, according to the legend already narrated at the beginning of the book, Saturn, frightened that one of his children would replace him, devoured them (53). Of course, it is true that Saturn is called Chronos in Greek, and that this means *time*; but this is hardly to the point here. The historical parallel of the older generation triumphing over the younger, of the mindless brutality of the years of repression which followed, is all in this picture. Byron's imagery in *Childe Harold* is of a piece with it:

Baron Francois-Pascal-mon Gerard, Louis VIII Robed in Ermine d Fleur-de-lys *(1815)*. *l.*

Goya, Saturn evouring his Children *820–23). Oil on plaster.*

But France got drunk with blood to vomit crime,
And fatal have her Saturnalia been
To Freedom's cause, in every age and clime. . . .

or more succinctly:

Can tyrants but by tyrants conquered be?

I make no apology for introducing a little light relief after this. Here is a children's puzzle from the time of Waterloo (54). Napoleon's Hundred Days account for 'peaceful Louis driven from France'.

THE ROYAL ALLIED OAK AND SELF-CREATED MUSHROOM KINGS

Behold the Oak, whose firm fix'd stay,
    Doth check Oppression's course,
Whose slightest branch can ne'er decay,
    While strong with Virtue's force.

Our much-loved Sovereign decks the branch,
    The highest of the Tree;
And peaceful Louis tho' driven from France,
    Among its boughs you'll see.

The Regent's Portrait next behold,
    Whose councils Wisdom guides;
And Russia's noble Monarch bold
    Who checked the Tyrant's strides.

Immortal Wellington next is seen,
    Whose fame can ne'er expire;
And veteran Blucher's warlike mien,
    That kindled Napoleon's ire.

The Mushroom Race you have to seek
    In weeds about the Root,
Who scarce dare at the Oak to peep
    Or at its Princely fruit.

54 A popular picture of 1815.

If you look at the picture you should be able to see the faces in the branches, but it is more difficult to work out what is hidden away in the undergrowth. I don't propose to make any heavy observations about the picture, though the fact that this was popular at the time might well be considered more convincing historical evidence than the thoughts of an anti-social avant-garde poet and an unbalanced Spanish artist.

7 Childe Harold Ventures Forth

In 1759 Dr Samuel Johnson published a novel, *The History of Rasselas*, in which an Abyssinian prince, brought up in isolation from the world in the remote and secluded paradise of the Happy Valley, determines to leave it in order to explore the mysterious world beyond its confines. He manages to make his escape, but after a series of inconclusive adventures in which his aspirations are seen to be merely 'phantoms of hope', he resolves to return to the Happy Valley; it is never made clear whether it was possible for him to fulfil this last wish.

As has often been pointed out, the story can be read as a satire on the Romantic movement, though written in advance of it. Certainly we could suggest that in our period it became fashionable to express dissatisfaction with the restricted world of normal behaviour, and to seek to break out from its enclosure, to venture beyond the limits of the known. The only way to do this in real life is by travel; and after all had not even Dr Johnson—usually, but falsely, seen as the epitome of the person who needs no additional information—had not even he made an expedition to explore the Hebrides?

Scotland

Scotland can claim to be pre-eminent among Romantic lands; it was also conveniently situated next to England, which provided the unromantic contrast. As George Gordon, Lord Byron, who is to be our guide in this chapter, announced in *Hours of Idleness* (1807):

> England! thy beauties are tame and domestic
> To one who has roved o'er the mountains afar;
> Oh for the crags that are wild and majestic!
> The steep frowning glories of dark Loch na Garr.

The scene in question is appropriately illustrated by Finden (55). Though Byron was recalling a visit made in his boyhood, he was also drawing upon an established literary tradition. It was not Byron who made Scotland Romantic; it was Sir Walter Scott.

Scott's works are largely unread today; yet there is a sense in which he is more Romantic than any of the other poets writing at this time. Certainly his influence on European literature was more far-reaching and perhaps more revolutionary than all the other poets put together, apart from Byron. After reading Percy's *Reliques of English Poetry* Scott—in a surprisingly modern way—went out to collect the surviving oral versions of the Border Ballads; these were published in 1802–3 as *The Minstrelsy of the Scottish Border*. This activity led him in turn to the writing of original verse romances, such as *The Lay of the Last Minstrel* (1805), and eventually to the series of novels which begins with *Waverley*. In his writings Scott explored the contrast between the Anglicized society of Lowland Scotland—the world of business and everyday reality—and the ancient feudal society of the Highlands. While at the lowest level this led to the production of Tartan souvenirs—and to George IV being seen in Scotland wearing a kilt—at an intellectual level it amounted to a new vision of history. Past ages were seen to have their own standards, instead of being judged by the limited morality of the present. In addition, it led to an appreciation of the national cultures and the revolutionary aspirations of suppressed minorities, such as the forgotten peoples who were subsumed in the vast empires of the Austria, Russia, and Turkey.

With these thoughts in mind, we embark on a brief tour of Southern Europe, following roughly the itinerary of *Childe Harold's Pilgrimage*. To each country that he visits Byron brings obvious preconceptions, and much of what he has to say seems very second-hand; his sentiments have been echoed by so many later travellers. Nevertheless, his journey shows an openness to experience which one cannot but admire.

55 Edward F. Finden, Lachin-y-Gair, *from* Finden's Illustrations of the Life and Works of Lord Byron, *(1833) Vol. 1 no. 4. Steel-engraving.*

The Orient

On 2 July 1809 the Falmouth Packet set sail for Lisbon; on board were nineteen passengers including Lord Byron, John Cam Hobhouse—a Cambridge friend with historical interests—and their three servants. Although the Napoleonic Wars were still in progress, it would be wrong to assume that twentieth-century conditions of total war prevailed. Byron might be seen as a young man of adventurous disposition attempting to make the conventional Grand Tour of Mediterranean lands which had formed part of an aristocratic Englishman's education in the eighteenth century.

Their first adventures were in Portugal and Spain, countries whose situation at that time has already been explained in the preceding chapter. The real object of the expedition was the Near East—the Balkans and Greece had been under Turkish rule for so long that to visit them was to visit the Orient. After leaving Malta, a British naval base, they penetrated Albania and were formally received at the court of Ali Pasha, Vizier of Janina; they were invited to Ali's castle at Tepelene, to see him 'finish a little war'. In making this visit Byron was already exploring beyond the normal bounds of English tourists, though he was protected by the goodwill of Ali Pasha. He described everything in a letter home:

> I shall never forget the singular scene on entering Tepaleen at five in the afternoon, as the sun was going down. It brought to my mind (with some change of *dress*, however) Scott's description of Branksome Castle in his Lay, and the feudal system. The Albanians, in their dresses, (the most magnificent in the world, consisting of a long white kilt, gold-worked cloak, crimson velvet gold-laced jacket and waistcoat, silver-mounted pistols and daggers,) the Tartars with their high caps, the Turks in their vast pelisses and turbans, the soldiers and black slaves with the horses . . .

Byron used this material in *Childe Harold II*, and identified himself with warriors such as these in poem after poem; he even purchased Albanian costume (56). It is very easy to laugh at this posing and dressing-up, but in Byron's case there is a real attempt to assume another personality, to commit oneself to other kinds of experience. (Incidentally, the costume shown in this picture still exists, and is displayed in the Bath Museum of Costume.)

The tour continued, and the travellers proceeded to Delphi and Athens. Years after Byron told Trelawny:

> Travelling in Greece, Hobhouse and I wrangled every day . . . He had a greed for legendary lore, topography, inscriptions; gabbled in *lingua franca* to the Ephori of the villages, goatherds, and our dragoman. He would potter with map and compass at the foot of Pindus, Parnes and Parnassus, to ascertain the site of some ancient temple or city. I rode my mule up them. They had haunted my dreams from boyhood; the pines, eagles, vultures, and owls, were descended from those Themistocles and Alexander had seen, and were not degenerated like the humans; the rocks and torrents the same. John Cam's dogged perseverance in pursuit of his hobby is to be envied; I have no hobby and no perseverance. I gazed at the stars, and ruminated; took no notes, and asked no questions.

57 Ruins of Hadrian's temple with a view of the south east angle of the Acropolis, and Parthenon, *from J. C. Hobhouse*, A Journey through Albania *(1813) p. 323.*

In fact the beginnings of his devotion to Greece are evident from this passage. Nor is John Cam Hobhouse's book to be despised; its illustrations give a fair if diagrammatic view of what Byron actually saw. This picture (57) clearly shows the mosque in the Parthenon. When the travellers inspected the temple more closely they observed the recent depredations of Lord Elgin, who had removed many of the sculptures. Byron was moved to attack 'the modern Pict' in *Childe Harold* II: Elgin could

> rive what Goth, and Turk, and Time hath spared

It was left to Hobhouse to point out the benefit which these marbles might confer on untrained English sculptors if they were exhibited in London. Neither of them thought of poets (see p. 109).

The contrast between the ruins and their surroundings began to come home to them: 'These noble masterpieces still retain their grandeur and their grace,' said Hobhouse, 'and towering from amidst their own ruins and the miserable mansions of barbarians, present a grand but melancholy spectacle'. As the journey continued through Asia Minor the presence of the Turks became more irritating; their barbaric justice and contempt for human life were everywhere prominent; and the romance of Tepelene never recurred.

56 Thomas Phillips, Byron in Albanian Dress *(1814).* Oil.

There are so many illustrations of Byron's Greece that one can only give a hint of the quality and the charm of the ruins from pictures like this (58). It is in fact earlier than Byron's visit by some years, but provides an apt parallel to

Fair Greece! sad relic of departed worth! . .

And yet how lovely in thine age of woe,
Land of lost Gods and godlike men, art thou! . .
Thy fanes, thy temples to thy surface bow,
Commingling slowly with heroic earth,
Broke by the share of every rustic plough: . . .

Childe Harold II, lxxiii, lxxxv

The turbaned Turks are either an additional charm or an intrusion, depending on one's point of view; and as Byron lingered in the country he began to share the dreams and hopes of the Greek patriots. In this he is as much the child of his age as was Wordsworth when he greeted the Spanish insurrection. Byron's poet in *Don Juan III* knew what he was doing when he sang:

The mountains look on Marathon—
    And Marathon looks on the sea;
And musing there an hour alone,
    I dreamed that Greece might still be free;
For standing on the Persians' grave,
I could not deem myself a slave.

Though poetry is often thought of as ineffective, these lines were to move generations of Philhellenes to overt political action. But in 1811 the time was not ripe; Byron returned to London. 'If I am a poet', he was later to say to Trelawny, 'the air of Greece made me one.'

Switzerland

When Byron resumed his wanderings in 1816 his fame was already secure; but this time he was committed to a life of exile which was to continue until his death. For the moment, at least, the conflict between the claims of marriage and society, on the one hand, and the inner life, expressed in the heroes of such poems as *The Corsair*, was resolved. In *Childe Harold* III,

> Self-exiled Harold wanders forth again,

resolved to explore new lands, and take from them, into himself, a reflection of the Romantic personality.

But first, in holiday mood, after passing through Belgium and Germany, Byron settled for a time on the shores of the Lake of Geneva (Lac Léman), where he was joined by the Shelleys. During a sailing trip round the lake they visited the castle of Chillon and saw the dungeon where François Bonnivard had been confined (59). This was not a subject

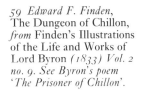

59 Edward F. Finden, The Dungeon of Chillon, *from* Finden's Illustrations of the Life and Works of Lord Byron *(1833) Vol. 2 no. 9. See Byron's poem 'The Prisoner of Chillon'.*

which at that time appealed to Shelley. But Byron was immensely impressed by the story: in the first place the good man imprisoned for political or religious reasons is a standard Romantic 'case'—one could, without too much twisting of words, call the political prisoner a Romantic image, since the literature is full of references to prisoners bursting their bonds. Consider too, Beethoven's *Fidelio*. Byron's prefatory sonnet speaks of the

> Eternal Spirit of the chainless Mind!
> Brightest in dungeons, Liberty! thou art . . .

but the effect of the whole tale is to cast some doubt upon this announcement—

> My very chains and I grew friends,
> So much a long communion tends
> To make us what we are:—even I
> Regained my freedom with a sigh.

In fact, the centre of interest in the poem is psychological—what is the effect of long imprisonment?—rather than exploratory of hope and liberty. The fact that Byron has put himself into the dungeon and imaginatively identified with Bonnivard lifts the poem above the level of sentimental tourism. It can be read as an allegory of the human condition.

The Alps

With what emotions would we expect the Romantic traveller to approach the Alps? Nature is more aggressive here than in England or Scotland; notice in Koch's painting (60) the diminutive human figures in the foreground; high above are the mysterious white peaks, alien and remote. Untouched by humanity, unpolluted, full of numinous meaning, the Alps seem to have 'issued from the hand of God'; their challenge is religious.

At first Byron, for all his scorn of the elder poet, could only trot out the most absurd sub-Wordsworthian rant:

> I live not in myself, but I become
> Portion of that around me; and to me
> High mountains are a feeling, but the hum
> Of human cities torture . . .

> *Childe Harold* III, lxxii

This is fit only for the lower slopes. Wordsworth himself had done better than this when describing his 1790 visit (*Prelude VI* and see p. 147) but this poem would not of course have been available to Byron and the others, apart from Coleridge.

60 *J. A. Koch*, The Schmadribach Falls *(1821–2). Oil.*

61 *J. M. W. Turner*, The Mer de Glace, Chamonix *(1802).*
Watercolour.

Turner's picture (61) shows the glacier below Mont Blanc, in the valley
of the Arve. This scene is central to English Romantic poetry; it is one of
the points where several poems 'meet' and a source from which whole
trains of imagery will flow. (In the preceding age of English poetry, the
Augustan, the comparable scene might be the Strand, London—a social
scene, 'the high tide of human existence'—not a barren wilderness like
this; it is necessary to appreciate this difference to understand how far we

have 'travelled'.) Coleridge contemplated this scene, admittedly in his imagination, and saw God in everything; his *Hymn before Sun-rise in the Vale of Chamouni* uses imagery which we have already encountered. Five torrents emerge from 'dark and icy caverns'; their 'invulnerable life' is 'stopped at once amid their maddest plunge'. In 1816 the Shelleys visited the same spot; it inspired the *Hymn to Mont Blanc*, and provided the setting of *Prometheus Unbound*:

> The crawling glaciers pierce me with the spears
> Of their moon-freezing crystals . . .

Here too, Mary Shelley placed the meeting between Frankenstein and the monster he had created:

> The sea, or rather the vast river of ice, wound among its dependent mountains, whose aerial summits hung over its recesses. Their icy and glittering peaks shone in the sunlight over the clouds. My heart, which was before sorrowful, now swelled with something like joy; I exclaimed—'Wandering spirits, if indeed ye wander, and do not rest in your narrow beds, allow me this faint happiness, or take me, as your companion, away from the joys of life.'
>
> As I said this, I suddenly beheld the figure of a man, at some distance, advancing towards me with superhuman speed. He bounded over the crevices in the ice. . . .

Consider also how Mary Shelley's novel begins and ends at the North Pole, another icy sea. (For the relation of this imagery to the sea of death, look again at Friedrich's *Arctic Shipwreck* (39).)

In a long descriptive letter to Peacock, Shelley described the frozen animals and gods that he imagined in this wilderness. One of them was Ahriman, the power of darkness in the Zoroastrian religion:

> Do you, who assert the supremacy of Ahriman, imagine him throned among these desolating snows, among these palaces of death and frost, so sculptured in this their terrible magnificence by the adamantine hand of necessity, and that he casts around him, as the first essays of his final usurpation, avalanches, torrents, rocks, and thunders, and above all these deadly glaciers, at once the proof and symbols of his reign . . .

'Final usurpation' here refers to Buffon's* theory; one day the glaciers would advance and cover the earth with ice; this would be the final catastrophe. To sum up, where the older generation of Romantic poets had seen God, the younger generation see the powers of destruction and death opposed to their Promethean dreams for the future of man. Byron, pressing on towards the high peaks, takes up the challenge:

> The clouds above me to the white Alps tend,
> And I must pierce them, and survey whate'er
> May be permitted, as my steps I bend
> To their most great and growing region, where
> The earth to her embrace compels the powers of air.
>
> *Childe Harold* III, cix

*Eighteenth century French naturalist—see picture (123).

Manfred

Byron's Journals of this year contain an account of his exploration of Switzerland:

> *September 22*
> Arrived at the foot of the Mountain (the *Yung frau* i.e. the Maiden); glaciers; torrents. . . .
> *September 23*
> Before ascending the mountain, went to the torrent (7 in the morning) again; the Sun upon it forming a *rainbow* of the lower part of all colours, but principally purple and gold. . . .
> Ascended the Wengen mountain. . . . On one side, our view comprised the *Yung frau*, with all her glaciers . . . on the other, the clouds rose from the opposite valley, curling up perpendicular precipices like the foam of the Ocean of Hell, during a Spring tide. . . .

These and similar observations form the scene for the drama of *Manfred*, which is set 'amongst the Higher Alps'. The story is similar in many ways to that of Goethe's *Faust*; Manfred summons up spirits which he is determined to control, because,

> The mind, the spirit, the Promethean spark,
> The lightning of my being, is as bright,
> Pervading, and far darting as your own,
> And shall not yield to yours, though cooped in clay!

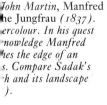

John Martin, Manfred *he Jungfrau (1837). ercolour. In his quest nowledge Manfred hes the edge of an s. Compare Sadak's h and its landscape).*

Though he is offered power, he cannot obtain oblivion, which he seeks in order to forget a nameless crime committed far in the past. He stands on the cliff near the Jungfrau, contemplating suicide (62). Martin's picture

conveys, as so often, the immensity of nature in contrast to tiny human figures (see also picture 111). The figure behind Manfred is that of a Chamois hunter, who saves him at the last moment.

Manfred reveals that his life's quest is to make himself equal to the gods and spirits. To meet them he ascends to the summit of the Jungfrau, with its 'glassy ocean of the mountain ice'. Here Manfred is taken up into the hall of Arimanes (i.e. Ahriman); he makes a request to be allowed to see again Astarte, his lost love. The phantom of Astarte appears, and foretells Manfred's imminent death. When Manfred does die, having rejected the consolations of religion, we are meant to feel that he is able to defy the spirits who come for his soul.

While the drama is unactable—one stage direction reads 'An eagle passes'—it seems to enshrine a number of themes and attitudes which are essential to any full acount of Romanticism. Of course, it is true that what Byron dramatizes is himself and his own inner life; but Manfred is not only Byron. In part he is Prometheus challenging the gods, and suffering on Man's behalf; in part he is Adam, trying to regain the innocent Paradise of the Golden Age before the Fall; in part he is Faust, in quest of forbidden knowledge. Finally, and in sum total, he is Man trying to break out of the limitations of the human condition by the exercise of his will. Though all these aspirations lead only to death, at least one feels that the path has been fully explored and the dangers confronted. Other poets, learning from this, will have to 'go round about', as Peer Gynt does in Ibsen's play; they will explore other paths, and endeavour to look beyond death itself. Byron, having made this attempt and survived, can face the future with humour and equanimity.

Italy

Italy might be considered to be the second homeland of the English Romantic poets. Wordsworth made three visits—though these are of little importance in the formation of his ideas—and Coleridge, after a spell of duty in Malta, travelled home through Italy in 1806. Scott and Keats came in search of health; in both cases it was too late, and Keats, as is well known, is buried in Rome. For Shelley and Byron, Italy was the land chosen for their exile; they found many of their compatriots already in residence.

In the years 1800–50 there was a general interest in Italy and a fashion for things Italian unparalleled before or since, even among the 'Italianate Englishmen' of the sixteenth and seventeenth centuries. Apart from the climate—on which see Byron's *Beppo*—there were several reasons for this. In the first place there were the obvious economic advantages for middle-class families in straitened circumstances; one could live well on

£150 a year. In the second place, it was a refuge from English 'respectability', that growing moral fervour which made it necessary for Byron and Shelley to leave England at this time. Thirdly, Italy offered scope for the indulgence of eccentric behaviour; we tend to forget how strange Byron's way of life seemed—even to Shelley:

> . . . Lord Byron gets up at *two*. I get up, quite contrary to my usual custom, but one must sleep or die, like Southey's sea-snake in 'Kehama', at 12. After breakfast we sit talking till six. From six to eight we gallop through the pine forests which divide Ravenna from the sea; we then come home and dine, and sit up gossiping till six in the morning. I don't suppose this will kill me in a week or fortnight, but I shall not try it longer. Lord B's establishment consists, besides servants, of ten horses, eight enormous dogs, three monkeys, five cats, an eagle, a crow, and a falcon; and all these, except the horses, walk about the house, which every now and then resounds with their unarbitrated quarrels, as if they were the masters of it . . . .

> After I have sealed my letter, I find that my enumeration of the animals in this Circean Palace was defective, and that in a material point. I have just met on the grand staircase five peacocks, two guinea hens, and an Egyptian crane. I wonder who all these animals were before they were changed into these shapes.

So much for those who say that Shelley had no sense of humour.

This letter was written from Ravenna, famous for the tomb of Dante. Several of our poets could speak or write Italian, and this again reflects a general interest in Italian literature. Our poets imitated Italian verse-forms: Byron's *Beppo* and *Don Juan* are written in *ottava rima*; his *Prophecy of Dante* and Shelley's *Triumph of Life* in *terza rima*. Both Shelley and Byron also translated excerpts from *The Divine Comedy*, and Blake illustrated the poem (see 109 and 132). Dante's fame increased steadily in England at this time, mainly because of new translations; H. F. Cary's blank verse rendering had a great influence on the work of Keats, in particular *The Fall of Hyperion*.

Politically, too, Italy excited widespread interest and sympathy among liberals. Byron was actively involved with the Carbonari, a secret society formed during the French occupation. The ideal of Italian freedom in the future contrasted with the melancholy relics of past glories which everywhere obtruded on the eye of the sensitive beholder. These form the subject of the fourth canto of *Childe Harold's Pilgrimage*.

Venice (63), the scene of the opening stanzas, had only lost her freedom in comparatively recent times; see Wordsworth's sonnet *On the Extinction of the Venetian Republic*. Byron's own lament seems rather drawn out in comparison, and in fact he spent most of his time in Venice enjoying himself in the spirit of *Beppo*. See Shelley's *Julian and Maddalo* for a particularly well-observed Venetian sunset. The Marlow picture (34) is also relevant here, since it confirms the link between London and Venice, cities founded upon trade and domination of the sea; it also

illustrates the contrast between them. Venice, in its decay, is one of the permanent habitations of the Romantic Imagination. As Byron said in a letter to Thomas Moore:

> . . . it has always been (next to the East) the greenest isle of my imagination. It has not disappointed me . . .

While we could have used Turner to illustrate Venice, it must be clear that a black and white version of an oil painting can convey very little. Nevertheless, in this case (64), we have a careful attempt to render the atmosphere, in both the literal and metaphorical sense, of Byron's Italy. The landscape stretches away into the distance, dotted with indistinct suggestions of ruin and decay. This is a 'poetic' evocation of the Roman Campagna, which relates to the idea of Italy suggested to Turner by the paintings of Claude. Compare Byron on the Italian landscape:

> Even in thy desert, what is like to thee?
> Thy very weeds are beautiful, thy waste
> More rich than other climes' fertility;
> Thy wreck a glory, and thy ruin graced
> With an immaculate charm which cannot be defaced.
>
> *Childe Harold* IV, xxvi

At the centre of this experience Byron placed the ruins of Rome itself.

The Ruins of Rome

Palmer's watercolour (65), done in 1838, shows the Roman Forum before modern excavation. The Colosseum can be seen in the background with

65 *Samuel Palmer,*
Ancient Rome *(1838).*
Watercolour. Uses two
viewpoints and combines
them; 'I was determined to
get the whole of the ruins,
which I believe has not been
done.'

66 *G. B. Piranesi*, Tomb of Caecilia Metella, a general view of the remains. *Etching from* Antichita Romane *(1756)* Vol III, Plate LI.

67 *G. B. Piranesi*, Nymphaeum in the gardens of Sallust. *Etching from* Il Campo Marzio dell' Antica Roma *(1762)* Plate XLIII.

the Sabine Hills beyond. Among the other monuments notice the single pillar of Phocas — 'Thou nameless column with the buried base' — which reappears in picture (124,v). Childe Harold, or rather Byron, conducts us round the principal Roman remains, such as the Tomb of Caecilia Metella (66). In Piranesi's engraving the tower is made to appear higher and more imposing than reality, but it matches well with Byron's stanza beginning,

> There is a stern round tower of other days

Compare the vegetation with that shown by Severn on the Baths of Caracalla (front endpaper).

Our problem is to sort out the merely 'tourist' impressions which Byron spills out in this strange enviroment, and to find the imaginative core of the poem. Byron said of Rome in a letter to Murray:

> As a *whole*, *ancient* and *modern*, it beats Greece, Constantinople, every thing — at least that I have ever seen. But I can't describe, because my first impressions are always strong and confused, and my Memory selects and reduces them to order, like distance in the landscape, and blends them better, although they may be less distinct.

Byron compares his own 'ruin' with the ruins of the past, and this, though it might seem puerile and counter-productive, in fact releases him from the burden of the 'quest' which has led him to drag 'the pageant of his bleeding heart' half-way round Europe:

> Upon such a shrine
> What are our petty griefs? — let me not number mine.

The poem continues with an astonishing stanza, describing the Palatine Hill:

> Cypress and ivy, weed and wall-flower grown
> Matted and mass'd together, hillocks heap'd
> On what were chambers, arch crush'd, column strown
> In fragments, chok'd-up vaults, and frescos steep'd
> In subterranean damps, where the owl peep'd
> Deeming it midnight; — Temples, baths or halls?
> Pronounce who can; for all that Learning reap'd
> From her research hath been, that these are walls —
> Behold the Imperial Mount! 'Tis thus the mighty falls.

> *Childe Harold* IV, cvii

In this apparent confusion lie the seeds of the method adopted in *Don Juan*, the adaptability of Byron's tone from sublime to jocular, the all-inclusive comprehensiveness of his approach to experience. The mysterious underground ruins find their counterpart once again in the work of Piranesi (67), who also suggests with his diminutive figures that

68 Henry Fuseli, The Artist moved by the Grandeur of Ancient Ruins *(1778–9). Red chalk and sepia. The fragments are now known to come from a colossal statue of Constantine.*

men are looking for significances which the ruins conceal. Further—and this looks ahead to Coleridge's use of Piranesi (see 112)—there may be an equivalent to Byron's stanza and this etching in the world of dreams; both suggest the cavernous depths of the subconscious mind.

Finally, Fuseli's sketch (68), showing the artist overwhelmed by the immensity of ruins which he can neither imitate nor comprehend, suggests the immense burden of the past, as well as the duty of the poet to confront the whole of human experience, and to make some sense of the historical process.

8 The Uses of History

In this section it is proposed to follow a parallel quest to that which occupied the previous chapter; but instead of looking for Romantic aspirations in other lands, we must now undertake a survey of human history with the same objective in view. While it is true that Byron, with his interest in the past grandeur of the countries he visited, was also travelling in time, in this chapter the most appropriate guide will be John Keats (69).

Keats has often been accused of trying on different styles of poetry, whether in imitation of Hunt, Milton or Shakespeare; this would imply that he never really found his own voice, except perhaps in the great Odes. It is also fair comment to point out that he avoids contemporary subject-matter in his narrative poems. In this he is at one with the fashions of the age in all senses, from women's clothing to styles of architecture and furniture design. If we concede that the Romantic Age was a revolutionary period, then, as in many newly established revolutionary states, people were in search of historical precedents for apparent novelties. At a deeper level, the conscious wish of artists to establish a school of historical painting, and of sculptors to emulate the Classical model, shows that fashion alone is not responsible for the interest in history.

Charles Brown, John
ts *(Summer 1819).*
cil sketch.

The Middle Ages

If we apply the standards of modern historical research, it soon becomes apparent that the Romantic poets knew very little about the medieval period. As we have seen, it was Sir Walter Scott who made the past come alive, and his novels were like a revelation to contemporary readers. And yet how wooden *Ivanhoe* (1819) seems today! In its own time it was an unprecedented effort of historical imagination, and must have seemed to be an accurate archaeological reconstruction. We, on the other hand, cannot accept the period detail of a work like *The Eve of St Agnes*; we are no longer interested in the authenticity of its supposed Middle Ages, but can try to understand why Keats chose that setting for his poem.

The less we know about a subject, the more scope it offers to the speculative day-dreamer to escape from the anxieties and stresses of the present. At this simple level the medieval period presented a vast theatrical wardrobe:

> Lo! I must tell a tale of chivalry;
> For large white plumes are dancing in mine eye. . .

So Keats begins one of his earliest poems, and soon makes it clear that he wishes to follow in the steps of Spenser. *The Faerie Queene*, archaic at the time of its composition, depicted a world of knights and ladies, wizardry and enchantment. An exact pictorial equivalent is not readily available from the sixteenth century, but consider this seventeenth-century painting (70) which was known to Keats.

We now know that this is a scene from the legend of Cupid and Psyche. Cupid asked Psyche never to look upon him, and visited her in darkness. When she broke this command he disappeared. Psyche is seen outside the Palace of Cupid, believing herself to be abandoned by him. By the late eighteenth century the 'story' of the painting seems to have been forgotten and it was known by its present title.

Keats used the painting as a stimulus to the imagination; it is probably the source of

> . . . magic casements, opening on the foam
> Of perilous seas, in faery lands forlorn.

> *Ode to a Nightingale*

It is clearly referred to in his *Epistle to John Hamilton Reynolds*, where it is the centre of a romantic reverie designed to cheer a sick friend:

> You know the Enchanted Castle,—it doth stand
> Upon a rock, on the border of a lake,
> Nested in trees . . .

> You know it well enough, where it doth seem
> A mossy place, a Merlin's Hall, a dream;
> You know the clear Lake, and the little Isles,
> The mountains blue, and cold near neighbour rills. . . .

The fantasies indulged in by other writers were hardly as innocent. In the late eighteenth century writers used the Middle Ages as a background to horror stories; in the same way that inter-planetary travel is used in science-fiction as a means of releasing the reader from normal social restrictions, so Gothic scenes were the appropriate background for narratives of wildness, sublimity and passion. Since time-travelling was not yet available as a convention in this type of fiction, nice English girls found themselves kidnapped by lustful monks, and were immured in

monasteries in some remote region of France or Italy. The most memorable example of this *genre* is *The Monk*, its author being subsequently known as 'Monk' Lewis. (Incidentally, this illustrates how impossible it was for anyone in Protestant countries to take monks seriously; they were either Friar Tuck guzzlers or villains in disguise, at least up to the Oxford Movement of the 1830s.)

The poets were aware of the crudity of these scenes; in the *Preface to Lyrical Ballads* Wordsworth attacks sensation-mongers who over-stimulate the imagination. Jane Austen parodies the novels and laughs at their readers in *Northanger Abbey*. But Keats had read Mrs Radcliffe's *The Mysteries of Udolpho*, for example, and one feels the *The Eve of St Agnes*, with its Gothic setting and hidden lover, is influenced by the conventions of this form of fiction, however he tries to refine them.

The third approach to the Middle Ages was archaeological—not of course the scientific study which we know today, but intensive, if uncritical, study of the churches, tombs and manuscripts which had survived. Blake had spent part of his apprenticeship drawing the tombs in Westminster Abbey. But in spite of the widespread interest in the subject, one must remember that even the basic sorting out of church architecture into Saxon, Norman and later periods had not yet been achieved. The situation is best illustrated by the phenomenon of Chatterton.

Thomas Chatterton (1752–70) produced poems which he said he had copied from manuscripts discovered in a chest at the church of St Mary Redcliffe (71) in Bristol. Many of the poems were by a 'new poet'—Rowley—who was supposed to have lived in the fifteenth century. The fact that these forgeries could have been accepted by educated people is indicative of the prevailing situation, and though Dr Johnson had exposed the 'whelp', the Romantic poets continued to admire him and valued his work. In producing late medieval verse Chatterton carefully avoided tell-tale Latinisms; the resulting poetry impressed Keats—'I always think of Chatterton when I think of Autumn'—and *The Eve of St Mark* fragment concludes with a remarkable piece of 'medieval' verse.

Other writers were influenced by the revival of the ballad form in Germany, which had originally been stimulated by the discovery of a collection of English ballads by Bishop Percy. This, with all the factors already mentioned, reverie, Gothic horror, and archaeological studies, combined in Keats' mind to produce *La Belle Dame Sans Merci*, thought by Rossetti and the Pre-Raphaelites to be the starting point of their movement. It was not, apparently, a poem which Keats thought worth preserving. This illustrates the deepening seriousness of the movement in the later nineteenth century, when the Gothic Revival in architecture, the Young England movement in politics, and the Oxford Movement in religion all went far beyond anything produced in our period. In the early nineteenth century it was still possible to treat the Middle Ages only half seriously, as in Peacock's *Maid Marian*; it is Mr Chainmail in *Crotchet Castle* (1831) who is the phenomenon of the new age.

> He is deep in monkish literature, and holds that the best state of society was that of the twelfth century. . . . He laments bitterly over the inventions of gunpowder, steam, and gas, which he says have ruined the world. He lives within two or three miles, and has a large hall, adorned with rusty pikes, shields, helmets, swords, and tattered banners, and furnished with yew-tree chairs, and two long, old worm-eaten oak tables, where he dines with all his household, after the fashion of his favourite age. He wants us all to dine with him, and I believe we shall go.

The Classical Heritage

Unlike medieval studies, the Classics were a school subject. Our poets all absorbed the Renaissance tradition that the writers of Greece and Rome were pre-eminent in the literature of the world, and that fluency in Latin and Greek was the mark of the scholar and the gentleman. I see no point in excluding Keats from this class, to which he obviously aspired. Although he could not read Greek, recent studies have shown how thorough his literary education was. In any case, Classical ideals dominated recent history; as Blake exclaimed

> The Classics! it is the Classics, & not Goths nor Monks, that Desolate Europe with Wars.

Although certain modern writers, such as Shakespeare and Milton, were thought to have equalled the Ancients, we find that the early eighteenth-century writers were keen to identify with the Augustan poets of Imperial Rome. In the middle and later periods of the eighteenth century, there was a revival of interest in the art and architecture of the ancient world which was backed by excavation and connoisseurship. This is usually described as Neo-Classicism or the Classical Revival. It often attracted quite different personalities to the 'Goths'; if the latter were often melancholy individualists, in some sense out of key with their own times, the Classical devotees on the other hand were representatives of the aristocracy and those eminent in public life throughout Europe. It is therefore difficult to see at first why such paintings as these (72, 73) were considered revolutionary in style and sentiment.

David has painted examples of patriotism from the early days of the Roman Republic. In the first picture (72) the three sons of Horatius, swearing to fight for their country, dominate the scene; the women are huddled away from the triumph of masculinity, symbolized by the straight lines, the weapons and the rigid poses. The overwhelmingly favourable reception given to this painting, which the artist said could not be finished in Paris, but only in Rome itself, shows the rejection of the lavish and frivolous culture of the French Court in favour of the martial virtues.

The second picture (73), painted in the year of the Revolution, deals with what had formerly been an example of moral rectitude of the highest order. This is the Brutus who drove the Tarquin kings from Rome and founded the Republic; he allowed his own sons to be executed because they had conspired against the new state. The relevance of this to the period of the French Revolution is obvious; 'through his Brutus as through his Horatii,' said a contemporary critic, 'David talks to the people more directly and more clearly than all the inflammatory writers whom the regime has confiscated and burned'. In its own day the

72 Jacques Louis David, The Oath of the Horatii *(1784–5). Oil.*

104

painting was much admired for its archaeological exactitude, and the fashions of the Revolution derive from this re-creation of the Roman world, including the hair-styles and the furniture. We can understand why the orators of the early Revolutionary period looked back to the Roman Republic and adopted its paraphernalia and titles. Napoleon became First Consul, and then Emperor; we can trace a comparable change in fashion.

While all this was taking place in France, German scholars and critics were pioneering a revival of interest in the Greeks. 'Greece!', Herder exclaimed, 'the youthful blossoming of the human race,—Oh that it could have lasted for all time.' This again is a comparable movement in that the virtues of what was thought of as a more primitive period are preferred to those of later and more decadent times.

The parallels in England must now be explored. The only significant poem about Roman virtue which we now remember is Wordsworth's *Laodamia* (1814); far more stimulating to the English poetic imagination was the vision of an ideal world. In the first place, this was derived from paintings by Claude; and it was expected that a landscape purporting to

show a Classical scene would look something like this picture by Turner (74). Archaeological accuracy was not the foremost requirement; what was wanted was a particular kind of atmosphere, which we might loosely characterize as serenity. Though the figures in this landscape seem incidental, it could be a scene from *Hyperion*, Book III. This vision of Classical times had been repeatedly illustrated throughout the eighteenth century, and it is hardly surprising that Turner, Keats (*Fragment of an Ode to Maia*), and Shelley (*Ode to the West Wind*) all invoke 'Baiae's Bay', near Naples, as an immediate and obvious 'touchstone' for the ideal Classical world.

Another well-known English view of the Classics was enshrined in pottery. At the Wedgwood showrooms (14) one could purchase elegant wares in the Neo-Classical tradition, claiming to have some relationship to originals from quite late Roman sources. Keats' narrative themes are often depicted in these plaques, which are of course much earlier than his poems. In our example (75), according to the modeller, Endymion is shown 'sleeping on the rock Latonius . . . . The dog, seeing the approach of Diana, barks and with his foot wakes his master.' In another plaque the Titans are compressed into a cave. We know that Keats admired Wedgwood, and there seems a strong possibility that designs like this may have been present in his mind when he begun to write.

Nevertheless, this is a cold creation compared to the rich fertility of *Endymion*, in which English plant-life seems to blend with and almost smother the vision of an early Greek era of patriarchal simplicity. A pictorial parallel is to be found in the engravings and lithographs of Edward Calvert (76), and in the work of Samuel Palmer. Calvert and Palmer share a vision of lush vegetation and Arcadian manners, set in a transfigured English landscape where, as Palmer's son tells us,

74 J. M. W. Turner, The Bay of Baiae, with Apollo and the Sibyl *(1823)*. Oil. *Exhibited with a quotation from Horace. Apollo granted the Cumaean Sibyl as many years of life as she held grains of sand in her hand; she did not ask for perpetual youth, and so wasted away until she became a voice.*

75 Wedgwood plaque, Endymion Sleeping on Mount Latmos *(c. 1790).* Blue Jasper ware with white applied figures; made in Etruria. Direct copy of a Roman bas-relief.

Edward Calvert, Ideal
storal Life *(1829).*
hograph 43 mm × 77
.

Spring clothed the innumerable orchards with clotted blossom, and Autumn never failed to fulfil this fair promise by lavishing the fruits in such profusion that the very leaves seemed in hiding, and the boughs were bent lower and lower till their treasure rested on the grass.

Later we shall consider Calvert's *The Cyder Feast* (87) as an analogue of Keats' Ode *To Autumn*.

Keats was not content to see the Greeks merely as Arcadian shepherds; they had also produced poets

> . . . bards who died content on pleasant sward,
> Leaving great verse unto a little clan . . .

Fragment of an Ode to Maia

Of the Greek Poets, Homer was pre-eminent. This had not always been the case. At the beginning of the eighteenth century Homer had been considered equal to the Latin poet Virgil; in their quest for original genius critics had turned away from the Romans. The reputation of Virgil, once thought of as an improver or polisher of Homer's barbaric glories, had now declined. By the end of the century Homer towered over all other ancient poets, whether Greek or Roman. Keats salutes the phenomenon of Homer in a famous sonnet; though he was unusual in beginning his Homeric studies with Chapman's version. If they had not been brought up on Pope, Keats' contemporaries would have read William Cowper's translation with illustrations by Flaxman (77). Notice the uncluttered freshness and the clarity of line. Otus and Ephialtes were not in fact Titans, but their subjugation of Ares might well be a scene from the war between gods and Titans which is the subject of Keats' *Hyperion*, his own attempt to write a poem of Homeric grandeur.

78 Slab XL (115–118) the Elgin Marbles. Ode on a Grecian Urn, iv: 'that heifer lowing at the skies.'

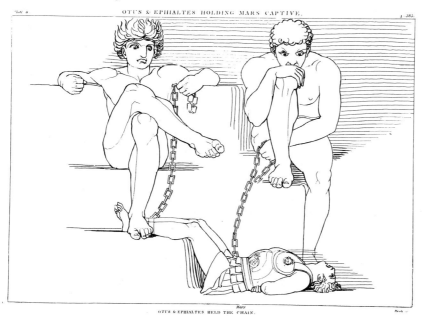

OTUS & EPHIALTES HOLDING MARS CAPTIVE.

OTUS & EPHIALTES HELD THE CHAIN.

77 John Flaxman, Otus and Ephialtes holding Mars captive, from the Iliad of Homer (1793). Engraved by Thomas Pirolli. The scene is from Book 5; Mars should strictly speaking be called Ares, the Greek god of War.

*Ascribed to John Keats,
the Sosibios Vase. Ink.*

While Keats was thinking about this poem he went to see the Elgin marbles (78), the sculptures which had originally adorned the Parthenon. This was his first experience of real Greek art; up to this time he had inevitably been forced to contemplate it through the filter of Neo-classicism. He wrote a sonnet *On Seeing the Elgin Marbles* which conveys the mental agony of contemplating

> . . . each imagin'd pinnacle and steep
> Of godlike hardship . . .

and by the intensive study of various examples of Graeco-Roman sculptured vases (79), he was able to create an imaginative synthesis in the *Ode on a Grecian Urn*. The procession from the Elgin marbles is present in the fourth stanza of the *Grecian Urn*, but so transmuted that it is no longer a question of sources and derivations; the pictures on the Urn become visions of an ideal existence. A similar vase is described at the beginning of the *Ode on Indolence*, and the Elgin marbles are again present in Book II of *Hyperion*, where the Titans seem fused with the 'couches of rugged stone' on which they lie. In spite of the condescending remarks of Byron and others, Keats does seem to make Greek art come alive.

Egypt

If the Classical world of Greece and Rome stood for beauty, truth and simplicity, Egypt symbolized mystery and the exotic. It had always been a country with a reputation for hidden knowledge, even to the ancient Greeks. The West still preserved Herodotus' attitudes, even his names for the Pharaohs. Under the Muslim occupation it had been a forbidden area, and it was Napoleon's expedition (80) in 1798 which first opened the country to modern exploration and the systematic looting which went by the name of Egyptology.

Napoleon had dreamt of emulating Alexander and arriving overland to confront the British in India. Actually his expedition ended in disaster, and its only immediate effect was a craze for things Egyptian which swept through Western Europe, as similar crazes, inspired by Tutankhamen, have in our own day.

This influence can be clearly seen in some of the furniture of the period (81); it was decorated with lions' or sphinxes' heads, lotus flowers and scarabs; claws often terminate the legs of tables and chairs. In *Lamia*, though the setting is meant to be ancient Greece, there is an element of Regency exotic in the description of the furnishings of Lamia's palace:

> Twelve sphered tables, by silk seats insphered,
> High as the level of a man's breast rear'd
> On libbard's paws . . . .

81 Belzoni, *the revised*
portrait issued by his widow
(c. 1824). Engraving. The
two colossal heads were
given to the British
Museum.

2 'Egyptian' style
urniture designed by
Thomas Hope (c. 1800–7).

The poets, however, were more fascinated by the images of grandeur
and mystery which the traveller's stories inspired. Keats listened to the
plans of Joseph Ritchie, and was pleased to think that the explorer was
carrying one copy of *Endymion* 'on a camel's back through the plains of
Egypt'. Byron knew William Bankes — 'the Nubian Discoverer'. The most
bizarre of all the explorers was Giovanni Belzoni, who is seen here in all
his glory (82).

The Greeks had identified a number of Egyptian colossi near Thebes
with the hero Memnon. Belzoni was determined to bring back the head
then known as Young Memnon to England; it was part of a group of
statues which had been shattered by an earthquake in 27 BC. With
incredible persistence Belzoni managed to persuade the local inhabitants
to help him move the head to the river on rollers. Long before the head
arrived in England (it is now in the British Museum), news of Belzoni's
activities had reached London. In 1817 Shelley competed with Horace
Smith in writing a sonnet on *Ozymandias*. There is some confusion here.
Ozymandias is the name of Rameses II in Greek history; and while the

head which Belzoni moved was in fact that of a statue of Rameses II, it is a neighbouring colossus which bears the inscription: 'My name is Ozymandias, king of kings; if any would know how great I am, and where I lie, let him surpass me in any of my works'. All this appears transformed in Shelley's sonnet: the 'shattered visage', the inscription, and the desolation—

> . . . Round the decay
> Of that colossal wreck, boundless and bare
> The lone and level sands stretch far away.

After his success with Memnon, Belzoni cleared the sand from the buried temple of Abu Simnel, discovered six tombs of Egyptian kings, and managed to open the Second Pyramid. This should have contained the body of Chephren, but the sarcophagus was broken and empty. Byron, transferring the scene to the First Pyramid, commented:

> What are the hopes of man? Old Egypt's King
>   Cheops erected the first Pyramid
> And largest, thinking it was just the thing
>   To keep his memory whole and Mummy hid,
> But somebody or other rummaging,
>   Burglariously broke his coffin's lid.
> Let not a Monument give you or me hopes,
> Since not a pinch of dust remains of Cheops.
>
> *Don Juan* I, ccxix

On his return to England, Belzoni exhibited his discoveries at the Egyptian Hall, Piccadilly, in the summer of 1821. The hall had been built in 1812 by Mr William Bullock to hold a collection of natural history. The façade must have been a familiar sight to our poets and the hall itself was used by Haydon to exhibit *Christ's entry into Jerusalem*.

All in all, Egyptian civilization made a contribution to Romantic poetry which has usually been disregarded. A quick check reveals four or five references in the first book of *Hyperion*, for example. The hieroglyphics were yet to be deciphered, and names and dates were frequently confused. Not everybody was as enthusiastic as Belzoni and his admirers; for De Quincey, in *Confessions of an English Opium Eater*, Egypt was the ultimate horror:

> I came suddenly upon Isis and Osiris: I had done a deed, they said, which the ibis and the crocodile trembled at. Thousands of years I lived and was buried in stone coffins, with mummies and sphinxes, in narrow chambers at the heart of eternal pyramids . . . .
>
> All the feet of the tables, sofas, etc., soon became instinct with life: the abominable head of the crocodile, and his leering eyes, looked out at me . . . .

One can have too much of anything. In 1824, shortly after Belzoni's death, his wife attempted to revive his exhibition. It was a failure. The fashion had come and gone.

9 The Poetry of Earth

The preceding two chapters were an attempt to follow the Romantic quest through space and time; the next two chapters will continue the exploration—into the heights of the air, and into the abyss below. For the moment we have reached a point of rest, an interlude; it is time to put aside the worry and the fret of human existence, and to look out of the window.

The Open Window

As one might expect, Friedrich's painting of an open window (83) is not as simple as it first appears. In many ways it would suit us better if it were

83 Caspar David Friedrich, View through a Window *(c. 1806). Wash.*

not loaded with Christian allegory; we are told that the farther shore of the river is paradise, that the dark room symbolizes our life in this world, and that the cross formed by the bars of wood in the top half of the window is a Christian symbol. (Friedrich used this allegory again in the painting *Woman at the Window*, so that we have a double check on this interpretation.) In English Romantic poetry there are also references which relate to Friedrich's allegory, in particular in Blake, who said that Man was confined in the Mundane Shell of the five senses, which obscured his vision; Keats, in the *Ode to Psyche*, ends with the thought of

> . . . a casement ope at night,
> To let the warm Love in!

and in the *Ode to a Nightingale* we are told that its voice

> . . . oft-times hath
> Charm'd magic casements, opening on the foam
> Of perilous seas, in faery lands forlorn.

(One might also consider the remarkable use of the symbol of the window as a frontier between life and death in Emily Brontë's *Wuthering Heights*.)

Leaving aside these metaphysical interpretations and allusions, there still remains the simple and literal level of 'meaning': Friedrich's window opens upon a landscape. I would like to argue that, although spiritual meaning may be present to Friedrich, and cannot be excluded in the discussion of such poets as Wordsworth and Coleridge, we have now arrived at a point in the history of ideas where landscape can be seen as an end in itself, and not as a symbol of something beyond itself. In this sense Keats spoke of the 'poetry of earth' which is 'never dead'; it is for this kind of poetry that many readers value the ode *To Autumn*, and the landscape paintings of John Constable.

The Hay Wain

The Hay Wain (84) is a familiar and much loved picture of the English scene. So much has it become a kind of national ikon that it is difficult to realize that Constable's works were as revolutionary in their day as the paintings of the Impressionists in the later nineteenth century. (It is interesting to note that Constable was more appreciated in Paris than in London, and that it is possible to trace his influence on later schools of French painting.) It is also true that Constable's more famous pictures are 'finished' works, and it may be easier to see what he is trying to do by examining his sketches, which are in any case more appealing to modern

John Constable, The
y Wain *(1821). Oil.
ginally exhibited under
title* Landscape: Noon.

taste; there is a study for *The Hay Wain* in the Victoria and Albert Museum. However, it was the finished pictures which were seen by his contemporaries, and so I have reproduced the final version of *The Hay Wain* here.

First of all, consider the subject matter. A farm cart is seen crossing a river; one of the two human figures (in the cart) appears to be addressing a remark to a dog on the bank (there was originally another figure in front of the dog and the fact that this has been painted out indicates how unimportant the 'human interest' must be). This takes up a very small area of the picture which otherwise consists of a cottage, some large trees, a distant scene of flattish country, and a large expanse of sky. I am deliberately being naive because I want to make you look at this picture as if for the first time. What exactly is the point of it?

The scene depicted is taken from the real world; it is not a close but an exact rendering of the buildings and the river near Flatford Mill on the Stour. In this area Constable grew up. Looking back, he said:

> . . . the sound of water escaping from mill-dams, etc., willows, old rotten planks, slimy posts, and brickwork, I love such things . . . . Painting is with me but another word for feeling, and I associate "my careless boyhood" with all that lies on the banks of the Stour; those scenes made me a painter, and I am grateful; that is, I had often thought of pictures of them before I ever touched a pencil.

The fact that this is a scene of childhood is one way to relate the picture to the poetry of the Romantics, in particular Wordsworth. *The Prelude* celebrates those 'spots of time' which endure in the memory and offer 'restoration' to the poet and his imagination in later life. While appreciating the force of this argument, one has to point out that there is nothing to indicate this in the painting itself; it does not seem to be a picture 'about Constable' in the way that Wordsworth's poems are very much 'about Wordsworth'. In this case the artist has been absorbed into his work.

Another interpretation of the 'meaning' of the picture is as follows. It is suggested that in Constable's major paintings there is preserved a 'moment of transition'; in this case it would presumably refer to the crossing of the river, and the admittedly rather unusual sight of a farm cart in the middle of the stream—though this would have seemed more usual then than now. This argument can be more easily substantiated from a picture like *The Leaping Horse*, where the horse is, as it were, caught in mid-air. It is then suggested that there is something very significant in the freezing of the action at the midpoint of the transition, that life is full of 'rites of passage', of rivers to be crossed. Once again, it is very difficult to see this in the tranquillity of Constable's painting.

To Autumn

Be that as it may, both the above arguments might equally be applied to Keats' *To Autumn*, though I think that they do not take us far into the heart of the poem. It can be said that in *Autumn* Keats presents the harvest of a life spent in observing Nature, and that a rich haze of memories hangs about the poem. Secondly, it is true that Keats is describing a moment of transition between summer and winter, and that he may—or may not—have felt that he was himself at such a transition in his own life. In answer, one can only read the poem again, perhaps alongside Thomas Hood's roughly contemporary *Ode: Autumn*; Hood is strongly influenced by Keats, but falls into the morass of subjective complaint which Keats himself avoids:

> The squirrel gloats on his accomplish'd hoard,
> The ants have brimmed their garners with ripe grain,
>   And honey bees have stored
> The sweets of Summer in their luscious cells:
> The swallows all have wing'd across the main;
> But here the Autumn melancholy dwells,
>   And sighs her tearful spells
> Amongst the sunless shadows of the plain.

                    Alone, alone,
                  Upon a mossy stone,
            She sits and reckons up the dead and gone
            With the last leaves for a love-rosary,
            Whilst all the wither'd world looks drearily,
            Like a dim picture of the drowned past
            In the hush'd mind's mysterious far away . . .

How different this is from Keats' Ode, and the general tenor of the remarks in Keats' letters of the same date, which seem to describe a scene like that in Lewis's picture (85):

> Since I have been at Winchester I have been improving in health—it is not so confined—and there is on one side of the city a dry chalky down where the air is worth sixpence a pint. . . .
> How beautiful the season is now—How fine the air. A temperate sharpness about it. Really, without joking, chaste weather—Dian skies—I never liked stubble-fields so much as now—Aye better than the chilly green of the Spring. Somehow a stubble-plain looks warm—in the same way that some pictures look warm. This struck me so much in my Sunday's walk that I composed upon it.

85 George Robert Lewis, Hereford, Dynedor and Malvern Hills from the Haywood Lodge, Harvest scene, afternoon 1815 *(painted c. 1817). Oil.*

86 Nicolas Poussin, Summer, *or* Ruth and Boaz *(1660–4). Oil.*

The reference in 'some pictures look warm' might well be to such works as Poussin's *Summer* (86), which was known to Keats. The alternative title to this picture is *Ruth and Boaz*, reminding us of

> . . . the sad heart of Ruth, when, sick for home,
> She stood in tears amid the alien corn.
>> *Ode to a Nightingale*

Calvert and Palmer

It is in the work of Edward Calvert and Samuel Palmer, the disciples of William Blake, that we find equivalents to the natural richness in Keats' poems. We have already seen how Calvert illustrates the pastoral and classical settings of *Endymion* (76); similarly, the Ode *To Autumn* is complemented by *The Cyder Feast* (87). The riotous and yet decorous dancers may seem to distract from the cider-making, yet the detail of the cider-press on the right-hand side is helpful in visualising 'the last oozings' in the second stanza of Keats' Ode. Calvert emphasizes the rich fertility of the orchard, and he indicates that he also saw mystical allusions of a Christian nature in this wood-engraving; the caption reads BY THE GIFT OF GOD IN CHRIST. If we look at Calvert's other pictures from the 1820s and 30s, we can see that they are intended to convey his vision of a Heaven which included the best of earthly existence; Calvert thought of Heaven as 'that serene kingdom, teeming with the good and the true and the beautiful'. This remark may or may not help us to understand the conclusion of the *Ode on a Grecian Urn*; we may also find Calvert's Christianity rather less obvious than his delight in the world of the senses; and we may feel, as Wordsworth did when he contemplated Keats' *Endymion*, that all we have here is 'a pretty piece of paganism'.

87 Edward Calvert, The Cyder Feast *(1828). Wood engraving actual size. First state.*

The next wood-engraving shows how much of Calvert's and Palmer's work springs from Blake's illustrations to Thornton's *Virgil* (88). It was in 1821 that Blake was asked to engrave a series of small blocks for Ambrose Philips' imitation of Virgil's first Eclogue. Though these tiny engravings did not impress Dr Thornton, who thought their technique crude, they contain a vision of a rural and patriarchal society which influenced Calvert and Palmer. Notice the word 'rest' in the following extract from Palmer's notes on the engravings:

> They are visions of little dells, and nooks, and corners of Paradise; models of the exquisitest pitch of intense poetry. I thought of their light and shade, and looking upon them I found no word to describe it. Intense depth, solemnity, and vivid brilliancy only coldly and partially describe them. There is in all such a mystic and dreamy glimmer as penetrates and kindles the inmost soul, and gives complete and unreserved delight, unlike the gaudy daylight of this world. They are like all that wonderful artist's works the drawing aside of the fleshly curtain, and the glimpse which all the most holy, studious saints and sages have enjoyed, of the rest which remaineth to the people of God. . . .

88 William Blake, 'Unyoked heifers, loitering homeward, low'. *Illustration from Thornton's* Virgil, *third edition (1821). Wood engraving actual size.*

Palmer's harvest scene (89), as so often in his work, takes place under the light of the moon, which we have already seen to be a symbol of the imagination. I can only allude to the enormous moons which so often hang in Palmer's skies; in his old age he was to lament 'the smaller modern moon' of the later nineteenth century.

Palmer also preached the doctrine of Excess, thinking of Blake's Proverb: 'The road of Excess leads to the palace of Wisdom.' In his notebooks he says that 'Excess is the essential vivifying spirit, vital spark, embalming spice . . . of the finest art.' In this he seems very close to the poetic ideal of Keats, who wished to 'load every rift with ore', and who created a strange world of buds, whorls and blossoms in his *Endymion*. 'Embalming' too, reminds us of the 'embalmed darkness' of the *Ode to a Nightingale*. That Palmer is the visual analogue of Keats needs little further proving, and *The Magic Apple-tree* (90) with its resting shepherd

89 Samuel Palmer, Harvest under a Crescent Moon *(1826). Wood engraving actual size.*

90 Samuel Palmer, The Magic Apple-tree *(1830). Watercolour.*

and sheep, its half-hidden spire and moonlit North Downs must stand here to represent the enclosed nest-like world of Palmer's vision. Keats, however, did not share Palmer's Christianity, and he also differed from Palmer politically. I think it is important to mention this apparently unrelated point, because one of the things which takes away from Palmer's greatness is his inability to sympathize with the sufferings and the political aspirations of the labourers who figure in his landscapes. He seems unwilling to allow his pastoral to merge with reality; but then the same might be said of almost any pastoral writer, and perhaps Keats is not exempt from this charge. Palmer's *The Sleeping Shepherd* (91) is

91 Samuel Palmer, The Sleeping Shepherd: Early Morning. *Etching, state iv. Plate 5 of* Etchings for the Art Union of London by the Etching Club *(1857). Palmer painted a similar* Sleeping Shepherd *in oil (1833–4).*

based upon a Graeco-Roman figure of 'Endymion the Shepherd Boy Asleep Upon Mount Latmos'; it therefore links the imaginations of poet and painter, and makes clearer than ever the idea of the 'rest' prepared for the people of God. But neither Keats nor Palmer had ever experienced the life of a real farm labourer; and when one appeared on the literary scene, offering himself for serious consideration as a poet, it was as if the figure in this picture stood up and spoke.

John Clare

John Clare's life is a case-history. The biographical information is relevant to the general themes of this book, because Clare's story illustrates what society could do with somebody who fulfilled many of the requirements of the ideal Romantic poet (see further in Chapter 12). Clare was born in 1793, and so was roughly a contemporary of Shelley and Keats; he came from the village of Helpston, originally in Northamptonshire and now in Cambridgeshire; like his father, he began by working as a labourer in the fields. After several attempts to publish his poetry locally, his first book—*Poems Descriptive of Rural Life*—was issued in 1820 by John Taylor, who was also the friend and publisher of John Keats. Clare's book was an immediate success, and he became widely known as 'the Peasant Poet of Northamptonshire'. Although there had been earlier examples of such hidden rural talent, Clare seemed to fit the Romantic concept of the poet inspired by Nature—and fortunate in his lack of formal education. It is at this time that the portrait was painted (92).

92 *William Hilton,* John Clare *(1820). Oil.*

For a time he was taken up by society, and became the object of well-intended charitable interest. The effect of this was to disorientate him completely; it was impossible for him to return to the life of a day-labourer; yet in the small village of Helpston there was nothing else for him to do. His later volumes of poetry were not successful, and there was in any case a general slump in the sales of verse after 1825. Later, after many years of poor health, he was placed in an asylum at High Beech in Essex; he ran away, and somehow found his way back home. Eventually he was certified insane; the certificate of application for his admission to Northampton General Lunatic Asylum, 28 December, 1841, has a section asking whether insanity had been preceded by 'any severe or long continued mental emotion or exertion'; his doctor gave the answer 'after years addicted to poetical prosing'.

He continued to write poetry until his death in 1864; much of it is still in manuscript. It is true that he suffered from delusions, and thought that he was Lord Byron giving the world further cantos of *Childe Harold* and *Don Juan*; but some of his later lyrics, in particular the 'I am' series of poems, have been preferred to much of his earlier work. Most of Clare's writings are less demonstrative, and show a patient observation of nature.

Natural Painture

At this point the argument returns to John Constable and the points already made about *The Hay Wain*. Can we find a visual analogue for the work of John Clare? *The Cornfield* (93) shows a country lane, probably in

93 *John Constable,* Th Cornfield *(1826). Oil. Exhibited as* Landscape Noon—*see (84)—with quotation from Thomson Seasons: 'a fresher gale Sweeping with shadowy gust the fields of corn.'*

late July. A boy, who is driving sheep, is taking a drink from the stream. The painting shows 'the lane leading from East Bergholt ... to the pathway to Dedham across the meadows, a quarter of a mile from East Bergholt Church, and one mile from Dedham Church, as the crow flies. The little church in the distance never existed'.

Here again, one could make many references to English Romantic poetry. For example, the poem by Wordsworth beginning 'There was a boy' describes a youth who 'blew mimic hootings to the silent owls': while listening for their reply 'the visible scene/Would enter unawares into his mind'. How much of what the drinking boy in the picture sees will return to him later in life, though he is unconscious of it now? Secondly, one could refer to the serenity of the scene and its relation to Keats' *Autumn*. But, as with *The Hay Wain*, neither of these references are exactly 'on target'. Constable himself said in a letter of 1802: 'There is room enough for a natural painture' (he actually wrote 'painter'), and continued: 'The great vice of the present day is *bravura*, an attempt to do something beyond the truth.' In a later letter he said:

> My limited and abstracted art is to be found under every hedge and in every lane, and therefore nobody thinks it worth picking up. . . .

What we have in Constable's work—and in Clare's—is a humility before Nature which makes much of the work of other painters and poets seem patronizing; the others are always trying to *use* Nature, to make it fit a theory about the Universe (Wordsworth), to illustrate a mood or symbolize a feeling (Byron, and much of Shelley and Keats). Clare and Constable report and describe what is there to be seen, assuming that this in itself is a valuable activity.

An admirer of Constable's wrote to him about *The Cornfield*:

> Sir, I think it is July in your green lane. At this season all the tall grasses are in flower, bogrush, bullrush, teasel. The white bindweed now hangs its flowers over the branches of the hedge; the wild carrot and hemlock flower in banks of hedges, cow parsley, water plantain, etc.; the heath hills are purple at this season; the rose-coloured persicaria in wet ditches is now very pretty; the catchfly graces the hedge-row, as also the ragged robin; bramble is now in flower, poppy, mallow, thistle, hop, etc . . .

Similarly Clare constantly lists what is there, as in *The Wheat Ripening*:

> What time the wheat field tinges rusty brown
> And barley bleaches in its mellow grey
> Tis sweet some smooth mown baulk to wander down
> Or cross the fields on footpaths narrow way. . . .

or in *Wood Pictures in Spring*, where he challenges the art of the painter:

The rich brown umber hue the oaks unfold
When springs young sunshine bathes their trunks in gold
So rich so beautiful so past the power
Of words to paint—my heart aches for the dower
The pencil gives to soften and infuse
This brown luxuriance of unfolding hues
This living lusious tinting woodlands give
Into a landscape that might breathe and live
And this old gate that claps against the tree
The entrance of springs paradise should be
Yet paint itself with living nature fails
—The sunshine threading through these broken rails
In mellow shades—no pencil eer conveys
And mind alone feels fancies and pourtrays.

To understand the boy in the picture, too, it might be better to forget Wordsworth and look at Clare's poems about rural youths, such as *The Driving Boy*.

'When I sit down to make a sketch from nature', said Constable, 'the first thing I try to do is, *to forget that I have seen a picture*'. Similarly, Clare's poems, especially the sonnets, which resemble 'sketches from nature', are now being presented to us in their original manuscript form, without the 'literary' finish which Taylor and his public required. 'The world is wide,' said Constable, 'no two days are alike, nor even two hours; neither were there ever two leaves of a tree alike since the creation of the world; and the genuine productions of art, like those of nature, are all distinct from each other'. In this spirit Clare, too, delighted in minute observation, and recorded what Blake called 'minute particulars'; later nineteenth-century writers, like Ruskin and Gerard Manley Hopkins, devoted years of their lives to the recording of the individual appearances of nature.

Enclosure

Implicit in the observations of all the writers and poets is a reverence for the English landscape, which is also seen as a secure and unchanging foundation for their life's work. Indeed, when one considers how much of the childhood of writers such as Wordsworth is interwoven in the memory with natural scenes, it could be argued that the scenery is almost part of their personalities. Therefore, to change the landscape in any drastic way is, in effect, to precipitate a psychic breakdown.

Luckily, the Lake District was not much affected by any large-scale changes; but in the Midland areas of England the enclosure of the common lands proceeded with some rapidity at this time, as improved methods of agriculture made it more profitable to reorganize the field-system and to enclose land previously thought of as heath or waste (94).

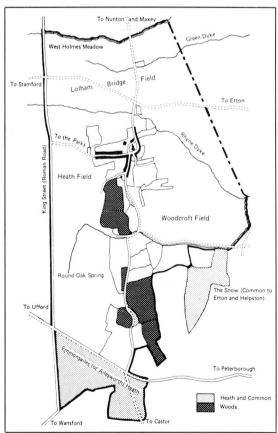

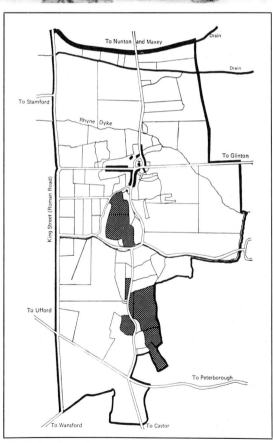

95 i & ii Two sketch maps of the parish of Helpston: (i) in 1809 before the enclosure;
(ii) in 1820 after enclosure. The scale is approximately 1 mile to 57 cm.

In Clare's own village, the two maps (95 i and ii) show the changes which took place between the Act of Enclosure for the village of Helpston (1809) and the final award (1820).

A good deal of what has usually been said of the effects of enclosure is now considered exaggerated. A whole class of small farmers were not dramatically plunged into poverty, and may in fact have been better off for a time. In Clare's case, for example, it is now known that he was able to earn more during the years of enclosure, by helping with fencing and planting, than he was at any other time. It is also fair to say that his psychological troubles coincided with the enclosure of Helpston, rather than being a direct result of them. But even with this caveat, there is plenty of evidence in the poetry which suggests that the destruction of the known and familiar landscape was seen as a crime against society and against the natural world, and not just a personal grief. The poem *Remembrances* is particularly relevant, but I quote only the penultimate stanza:

> By Langley bush I roam but the bush hath left its hill
> On cowper green I stray tis a desert strange and chill
> And spreading lea close oak ere decay had penned its will
> To the axe of the spoiler and self interest fell a prey
> And crossberry way and old round oaks narrow lane
> With its hollow trees like pulpits I shall never see again
> Inclosure like a buonaparte let not a thing remain
> It levelled every bush and tree and levelled every hill
> And hung the moles for traitors—through the brook is running still
> It runs a naked stream cold and chill

To visualize this we have only to imagine revisiting the lane in Constable's *The Cornfield* and finding things changed or destroyed—for example, the stile in the foreground, which seems to serve no useful purpose. Compare a prose note of Clare's:

Wed 19 Sept 1824. Took a walk in the fields saw an old wood stile taken away from a favourite spot which it had occupied all my life the posts were overgrown with Ivy & it seemed so akin to nature & the spot where it stood as tho it had taken it on lease for an undisturbed existance it hurt me to see it was gone. . . .

A Rural Ride

A similar melancholy pervades the later pictures of John Constable; in his case the personal sorrow of his wife's death is responsible for the

96 John Constable, The Mound of the City of Old Sarum, from the south *(1834)*.
Watercolour.

general feeling of sadness. But *Old Sarum* (96), while fully justified in its
own right for inclusion here as a work of art illuminating yet another
aspect of the Romantic poetry of earth, of ruin and decay, of the city
turned into a landscape, provides us with a transition to the themes of the
next chapter. Constable's own notes on the picture show his awareness of
these different levels of meaning.

> This subject, which seems to embody the words of the poet, 'Paint me a
> desolation', is one with which the grander phenomena of nature best accord.
> Sudden and abrupt appearances of light—thunder clouds—wild autumnal
> evenings—solemn and shadowy twilights 'flinging half an image on the straining
> sight'—with variously tinted clouds, dark, cold, and grey—or ruddy and bright—
> even conflicts of the elements heighten, if possible, the sentiment which belongs to
> it.
>   The present appearance of Old Sarum, wild, desolate, and dreary, contrasts
> strongly with its former splendour. This celebrated city, which once gave laws to
> the whole kingdom and where the earliest Parliaments on records were convened
> can only now be traced by vast embankments and ditches, tracked only by sheep-
> walks. 'The plough has passed over it. . . .'

The picture, said Sir Thomas Lawrence, should be dedicated to the
House of Commons; for it was not for its melancholy that Old Sarum had
become notorious. Throughout our period it returned two members to
Parliament, while some of the new manufacturing towns had no

representation. For a discussion of this in contemporary literature, see *Melincourt*, a novel by Thomas Love Peacock, in particular Chapters XXI and XXII—'The City of Novote' and 'The Borough of Onevote'; and, to refer in conclusion to a voice whose strident tones would have disturbed this brief interlude of rest, consider the opinions of William Cobbett, the author of *Rural Rides*.

Cobbett's value as a witness of rural conditions at this time may be debated; one fact, however, cannot be denied: at least he rode out and saw what was there. His descriptions of poverty on the one hand, and greed on the other, illuminate the background to the Captain Swing revolt of the 1820s and 30s, when distressed labourers burned the ricks of their employers. Here is an extract from a rural ride which passed by Old Sarum:

> When I came down to STRATFORD DEAN, I wanted to go across to LAVERSTOKE, which lay to my left of Salisbury; but just on the side of the road here, at Stratford Dean, rises the ACCURSED HILL. It is very lofty. It was originally a hill in an irregular sort of sugar-loaf shape: but, it was so altered by the Romans, or by somebody, that the upper three-quarter parts of the hill now, when seen from a distance, somewhat resemble *three cheeses*, laid one upon another; the bottom one a great deal broader than the next, and the top one like a Stilton cheese, in proportion to a Gloucester one. I resolved to ride over this ACCURSED HILL. As I was going up a field towards it, I met a man going home from work. I asked how he *got on*. He said, very badly. I asked him what was the cause of it. He said the *hard times*. 'What *times*,' said I; 'was there ever a finer summer, a finer harvest, and is there not an *old* wheat-rick in every farm-yard?' 'Ah!' said he, '*they* make it bad for poor people, for all that.' '*They?*' said I, 'who is *they?*' He was silent. 'Oh, no! my friend,' said I, 'it is not *they*; it is that ACCURSED HILL that has robbed you of the supper that you ought to find smoking on the table when you get home.' I gave him the price of a pot of beer, and on I went, leaving the poor dejected assemblage of skin and bone to wonder at my words.
>
> The hill is very steep, and I dismounted and led my horse up. Being as near to the top as I could conveniently get, I stood a little while reflecting, not so much on the changes which that hill had seen, as on the changes, the terrible changes, which, in all human probability, it had *yet to see*, and which it would have greatly *helped to produce*. It was impossible to stand on this accursed spot, without swelling with indignation against the base and plundering and murderous sons of corruption. I have often wished, and I, speaking out loud, expressed the wish now; 'May that man perish for ever and ever, who, having the power, neglects to bring to justice the perjured, the suborning, the insolent and perfidious miscreants, who openly sell their country's rights and their own souls.'

With these sentiments at least one of our poets would concur: let us examine the political poetry of Shelley.

10 The West Wind

The year 1819 is remarkable in many ways; it is the year of the Ode *To Autumn*, but also of the *Ode to the West Wind*; and it is also the year of Peterloo, a watershed in English political history. Percy Bysshe Shelley, exiled in Italy but eagerly following the news from England, summarized the state of affairs in the following sonnet:

> An old, mad, blind, despised, and dying king,—
> Princes, the dregs of their dull race, who flow
> Through public scorn,—mud from a muddy spring,—
> Rulers who neither see, nor feel, nor know,
> But leech-like to their fainting country cling,
> Till they drop, blind in blood, without a blow,—
> A people starved and stabbed in the untilled field,—
> An army, which liberticide and prey
> Makes as a two-edged sword to all who wield—
> Golden and sanguine laws which tempt and slay;
> Religion Christless, Godless—a book sealed;
> A Senate,—Time's worst statute unrepealed,—
> Are graves, from which a glorious Phantom may
> Burst, to illumine our tempestuous day.
>
> *Sonnet: England in 1819*

Before exploring the references in this poem we should perhaps look first at its author, and consider his qualifications as a writer of political verse.

Portraits of Shelley

Only two portraits of Shelley are known, and their authenticity can be questioned. In the first place, there is the well-known painting by Amelia Curran; the general sense of this portrait is preserved by Joseph Severn in *Shelley Writing 'Prometheus Unbound' in the Baths of Caracalla* (front endpaper), so that I do not reproduce it here. It must also be remembered that the artist was not herself satisfied; she was an amateur, and allowed

*Edward Ellerker Williams,
[Perc]y Bysshe Shelley
[182]1–2). Watercolour
[sketc]h.*

*[S]. H. Grimm, Field Place,
[Warn]ham, Sussex (1788).
[Wat]ercolour drawing.*

her work to be taken over by George Clint. But we may say, in all fairness, that her picture shows a Romantic ideal of a young poet.

While the Williams sketch (97) is also amateur, and leaves much to be desired, it does seem more like a real man. Its date is two years later than the Curran portrait, but the sitter looks more in keeping with his chronological age; before he died Shelley was beginning to go grey. Thomas Love Peacock, who knew Shelley well before he went to Italy, was not satisfied with any of the attempts to represent Shelley's features. One would expect to see an intensity of energy comparable to that which animated the poet's conversation, of which Peacock's novels provide the best record.

Political Expectations

Shelley was born on 4 August, 1792 at Field Place, Warnham (98), about four miles north-west of Horsham in Sussex. In showing this picture I am trying to establish Shelley's social position, and the expectations he inherited. The house is an imposing eighteenth-century gentleman's residence; its general appearance remains unchanged, though a portico was added in 1846. Shelley was born in the upper front room of the right-hand wing of the building. Field Place should remind us that Shelley was not always a wanderer and an exile; he was by birth and origin a country gentleman.

Shelley's family was what used to be called a 'county' family, and the picture helps us to appreciate the status of such an influential rank in society, as well as the income needed to maintain this position. Shelley's grandfather, Bysshe Shelley, who became a baronet in 1806, had twice married for money; he amassed a large fortune, said to be in the region of £200,000. (This would be a hundred times as much in today's money.) Like many eighteenth-century magnates, he was determined that the bulk of this fortune should remain intact; his estate was therefore entailed through the male line, so that his eldest son was compelled to pass on the estate to *his* eldest son. Percy Bysshe Shelley had the good luck to be born at the receiving end of this chain of inheritance; although his father quarrelled with him when he was eighteen, Shelley could not be disinherited, and was always able to raise money on his future prospects.

Such a family might well have figured in the pages of Jane Austen's novels; as members of the upper gentry, they had a clear role to play in the social system—they were expected to exercise their abilities in the field of politics. In the days before the Reform Bill many Parliamentary seats were in the gift of great noblemen; the Shelleys were under the patronage of the Whig Duke of Norfolk, who lived at Arundel Castle in Sussex, and controlled several of the neighbouring constituencies. Shelley's grandfather was made a baronet for political services, and Timothy Shelley, the poet's father, was the Member of Parliament for New Shoreham. It was naturally assumed that the Duke would arrange something similar for Timothy's son when he came of age; he might perhaps have been made the M.P. for Horsham.

All this is usually forgotten in assessing Shelley's contribution to political debate, and we naturally assume that the angelic poet, whom we substitute for the real Shelley, could never have accepted a Parliamentary seat on such terms. But it is worth noting that after quarrelling with his father in 1811, Shelley paid a visit to the Duke to ask for help; although he had become a Protestant, the eleventh Duke of Norfolk retained the Catholic sympathies of his family, and Shelley's strange visit to Ireland in 1812, with its accompanying distribution of political tracts, may be more than a coincidence. In assessing Shelley's later political activities, notice should be taken of the tract entitled *A Philosophical View of Reform*; this is not 'wildly revolutionary', and is useful corrective reading for those who think that Shelley was immature; had he lived to see the Reform Bill, he might well have been returned to Parliament as a moderate Liberal. Politics was the job for which his family background and training had prepared him, and the subject, directly or indirectly, of much of his poetry.

The King

Shelley's sonnet on *England in 1819* first deals with 'an old, mad, blind, despised, and dying king'. While the Prince Regent had for many years exercised the Royal powers and privileges, his father still lived on in an obscure corner of Windsor Castle. Shelley sees the mad king as the root of the situation, an embodiment of the worst kind of anarchy. The truth is more complicated.

George III had come to the throne in 1760; periodic bouts of 'madness' had led to earlier crises, from which the King had recovered. (Medical authorities are now inclined to believe that the King's illness was physical in origin, probably a form of porphyria.) In 1811, at the age of seventy-three, his personal rule came to an end, and a Regency was declared. The King was subjected to the usual treatment for madness; he was bled, purged, and placed in a strait-jacket. Soon he became totally deaf and blind; he grew a long white beard, and wandered about the castle in a purple dressing-gown. Nevertheless, he continued to live in the world of his imagination; he was sometimes to be found at the harpsichord singing to himself. He compared himself to King Lear (99);

99 *Joseph Lee*, George III as an Old Man *(c. 1815)*. *Enamel.*

indeed, he never forgot that he was the King, and endured his atrocious treatment with dignity. Even the Prince Regent, on hearing his father quote from *Samson Agonistes* the lines referring to blindness—'Oh dark, dark, dark, amid the blaze of noon . . .', was moved to pity.

Of course, this is not the whole story. Cobbett, as we might expect, saw the whole Royal Family as a burden upon the nation, and, after the King's death, Byron imagined the scene at Heaven's gate in *The Vision of Judgment*. The case for the prosecution is clear; George cannot be admitted to the rewards of the just because of the record of his government:

> He ever warred with freedom and the free.
> Nations as men, home subjects, foreign foes,
> So that they uttered the word Liberty,
> Found George the Third their first opponent. . . .

but the whole poem must be read; popular feeling, as shown in this broadsheet (100), must be contrasted with Byron and Shelley. Byron preserves a balance in his poem, which is really more concerned with the idiocies of Robert Southey, the Poet Laureate. In fact, in the last stanza, there is a kind of forgiveness, and a similar musical conclusion to that in the broadsheet ballad:

> All I saw farther, in the last confusion,
> Was, that King George slipp'd into heaven for one;
> And when the tumult dwindled to a calm,
> I left him practising the hundredth psalm.

100 *J. Harrold of Hinckley,* Elegy *(1820). Broadsheet. An example of the popular culture of the period.*

101 *Sir Thomas Lawrence,* The Prince Regent in Garter Robes *(1819). Oil.*

The Regent

Over the Prince Regent opinions differ. Some, like Shelley and most of his liberal friends, before and since, find it difficult to say anything good about him. Indeed, the contrast between the official portrait (101) and the image of the cartoonists (102) needs no comment. Cruikshank shows the Prince's life in outline: firstly, the young Florizel; secondly, the dissipated figure forever transfixed in Leigh Hunt's description—'a fat Adonis of fifty'; and thirdly, the builder of Brighton Pavilion—the Chinese folly surmounts a corpulent, if not gouty, Regent. On the Prince's side it can be argued that for many years he was excluded from office by his father, and therefore found himself with nothing to do; one can also make a good case for him as a man of intelligence and taste, which found expression in the plans for the redevelopment of London, carried through by John Nash (see further p. 183). The 'Regency period' still implies a particular kind of elegant taste in architecture, furniture and interior decoration, in fact the whole cultural milieu in which the younger Romantics grew up; but how far the Regent himself was responsible is a matter of opinion. Certainly he had some taste in literature, as is proved by his fondness for the works of Jane Austen: *Emma* is dedicated to him. His coronation can only be described as a scene from Sir Walter Scott.

One final note on the Lawrence portrait. Many years later Joseph Severn and George Richmond were visiting St John Lateran in Rome; they noticed a number of people in exaggerated attitudes of prayer in front of an enormous portrait. It was, of course, this picture of George IV. It had been given to the Vatican, and then placed in the church during a time when its usual home was being cleaned and decorated. The common people thought they had been given a new saint.

103 Dreadful scene at Manchester meeting of Reformers 16 August 1819. *Coloured print.*

Peterloo

The rest of Shelley's sonnet is best illustrated by this engraving of Peterloo (103). The cause of Parliamentary Reform has no more famous martyrs than those who lay dead on this 'untilled field'. The Reformers, as can be seen from their banners, wanted Universal Suffrage and Annual Parliaments; but their large numbers on this occasion, together with the suspicion that their 'drilling' was not only designed to ensure good order, provoked the local magistrates into reading the Riot Act and ordering the Yeomanry to charge. A few relics of the occasion, such as a banner with the inscription UNITY AND STRENGTH, and the top of a banner pole proclaiming HUNT AND LIBERTY, still survive in the Public Library at Middleton, Lancashire. As might be expected, the Regent sent a congratulatory message on 'the preservation of public tranquillity'. Lord Sidmouth, the Home Secretary, at first wished to praise 'the deliberate, spirited manner in which the magistrates discharged their arduous and important duty on that occasion. ... It may be deemed a matter of surprise and congratulation that the casualties have not been more numerous.' Though the letter was not published, his public statements were of the same kind. The repressive Six Acts were rushed through Parliament, and were generally linked with the names of Sidmouth, Eldon (the Lord Chancellor), and Castlereagh. All these are leading figures in Shelley's commemorative poem, *The Mask of Anarchy*, which was considered so libellous and inflammatory that it could not be published until 1832; with its companion poems, such as the *Song to the Men of England*, it had great influence on the Chartist movement of the thirties and forties.

Skiey Imagery

Up to this point I have tried, literally and metaphorically, to keep close to the ground, and to establish a real context as the occasion for such poems as the *Ode to the West Wind*. The difficulty—and it is a real difficulty in reading Shelley—is that once he has begun to write, he ceases to employ 'the language of men' (in saying this I am deliberately setting to one side such poems as the *Letter to Maria Gisborne* which are written in an urbane and conversational style). There are several reasons for this: one is that much of his poetry is in a mode which one can only describe as 'sublime', using the word in its eighteenth-century technical sense; such poetry was often thought good even if it were obscure, a precedent being ultimately derived from the Odes of the Greek poet Pindar. A second point to establish is this: as I have already suggested, Shelley, as a second generation poet, can attempt to write in a kind of rapid shorthand, relying on our previous acquaintance with Romantic poetry; in fact, he *thinks* in symbols, and it will not profit us much to try to tie these down to literal fact.

For example, Shelley will take over the boat from 'The Voyage of Life', and use it constantly. This we have already noted, but it is often rather alarming to find it transformed into an 'aerial car', allowing the poet, as in *Queen Mab*, to explore the heavens. We tend to forget that flight was not impossible at this time, as the picture of early hot air balloons (104) should remind us. Shelley was drawing upon human experience. The fact that balloons, like boats, are at the mercy of the wind, accounts for the apparent helplessness and aimlessness of Shelley's mental voyages, and need not be explained by a lack of masculinity and drive in his character.

Shelley conveys this feeling—of being adrift in an imaginary balloon—in his poem *The Cloud*. (Although as a piece of verse-making it seems to suffer from the rollicking rhythm, one could argue that this is a rapidly moving 'congregation of vapours'.) The poem is usually dated to 1820, possibly to the next year, and it provides a splendid illustration of Shelley's theory that all poets and artists are simultaneously affected by 'the Spirit of the Age'.

It was roughly at this time that the new science of meteorology was born. Luke Howard (1772–1864) kept detailed weather observations over a period of many years. In 1803 he read a paper on *The Modification of Clouds*, in which he described the nature and height of different kinds of clouds, giving them names such as cirrus and cumulus which are still in use today. The first volume of his study of *The Climate of London* was published in 1818. In Germany Goethe had already begun to work on clouds, but was greatly stimulated by Howard's book; he kept a record of the daily appearance of clouds for six weeks in 1820. Meanwhile, John

Montgolfier brothers demonstrating the hot air balloon at Versailles 19 September 1783. *Print*.

Cloud study *(c. 1822–5).*
Oil sketch.

Constable, the miller's son, who had always taken special care to get the clouds 'right' in his paintings, began to make studies of the clouds and sky (105); there are fifty such sketches from 1822 alone.*

How much of all this is coincidence, and how much the normal circulation of new ideas may be debated. We are more concerned with the cloud as a Romantic symbol. Wordsworth, for example, requests in the opening of *The Prelude* that,

> . . . a cloud shall point me out my way . . .

and the mysteriousness of the Leech-gatherer is enhanced by the description,

> Motionless as a cloud the old man stood,
> That heareth not the loud winds when they call;
> And moveth all together if it move at all.

The infant child comes 'trailing clouds of glory' in the *Ode: Intimations of Immortality*; a point which Coleridge answers in *Dejection* by suggesting that 'from the soul itself must issue forth . . . a fair luminous cloud/Enveloping the Earth'. Shelley in *Mutability* announces simply:

---

*Constable is not alone in this. Turner and Samuel Palmer, for example, also kept 'skying' sketchbooks for long periods. This is partly related to the observation of light already discussed in Chapter 4.

138

We are as clouds that veil the midnight moon . . .

The problem is to find anything in common between these and similar comparisons. Looking at John Constable's clouds, and trying to see shapes in them, would also be a profitless activity: one is reminded of the dialogue between Hamlet and Polonius on the subject—'Very like a whale'.

Nevertheless, the exercise enables us to arrive at some tentative conclusions about Romantic symbols. We must not expect to find allegory or fixed meaning behind them; not all rivers will be rivers of life, the sea will change its significance as will the moon, and there will be different associations in different contexts. What is Romantic is the consistent use of such fluid, changeable and amorphous shapes to 'body forth' the discoveries of the imagination. Of all these the cloud is the most variable, both in nature and in poetic 'meaning'. There are, in any case, many different kinds of clouds.

The Storm

It is for this reason, I think, that the second stanza of the *Ode to the West Wind* has been so often misunderstood.

> Thou on whose stream, mid the steep sky's commotion,
> Loose clouds like earth's decaying leaves are shed,
> Shook from the tangled boughs of Heaven and Ocean,
>
> Angels of rain and lightning: there are spread
> On the blue surface of thine aëry surge,
> Like the bright hair uplifted from the head
>
> Of some fierce Maenad, even from the dim verge
> Of the horizon to the zenith's height,
> The locks of the approaching storm. Thou dirge
>
> Of the dying year, to which this closing night
> Will be the dome of a vast sepulchre,
> Vaulted with all thy congregated might
>
> Of vapours, from whose solid atmosphere
> Black rain, and fire, and hail will burst: oh, hear!

The first sentence describes a most unusual cloud-formation, which it may be difficult to visualize. Here is a modern photograph taken in Wales (106); notice first the small clouds travelling ahead of the main body—

. . . loose clouds like the earth's decaying leaves . . .

and at the top of the picture the strange effect of the anvil-shaped thunder-cloud which can resemble hair being blown forward—

> . . . uplifted from the head
> Of some fierce Maenad.

The smaller clouds often appear to be shed by the larger one, and the idea of a 'stream' of leaves is not at all fanciful.

The second sentence prophesies the storm itself in apocalyptic terms; in considering the symbolic meaning of the storm to the Romantics one must first make the obvious comparison to war and revolution. Shelley sees political catastrophe in the near future, and he summons up the Spirit of the Age yet to come:

> The great writers of our age are, we have reason to suppose, the companions and forerunners of some unimagined change in our social condition or the opinions which cement it. The cloud of mind is discharging its collected lightning . . . .
> Preface to *Prometheus Unbound*

On a more personal level—and think here too of Coleridge's *Dejection: An Ode*—the storm is also a potential source of inspiration. The wind that blows through it can revivify the poet, and drive his 'dead thoughts' to 'quicken a new birth'; but implicit in Shelley's poem is the onset of danger and death. The forces which the poet requests to serve him are beyond his control.

Shipwreck

The West Wind is a destroyer as well as a preserver; a 'Wild Spirit',

> For whose path the Atlantic's level powers
> Cleave themselves into chasms . . .

*J. M. W. Turner,
The Shipwreck (1805).*

Such a force will have scant regard for human life! Romantic painting is full of similar images of disaster, and to select only one of Turner's catastrophes at sea is hardly to do him justice. Although *The Shipwreck* (107) can be praised for its epic treatment, it is important in the first instance not to see this as some sort of fictional event. To the contemporary beholder this subject would be as real as an air disaster would be to us today, and one has only to recollect the death of Wordsworth's brother in the *Earl of Abergavenny* (1805) to drive home such a parallel. Wordsworth's *Elegiac Stanzas* on this occasion were suggested by Sir George Beaumont's picture of *Peele Castle in a storm*, which shows 'a labouring hulk' drifting helplessly towards a lee shore. (Beaumont's painting does not reproduce well, but may be seen in Leicester Museum & Art Gallery; both painting and poem are related to the Voyage of Life sequence in Chapter 5.) Shelley's own death, on the other hand, is not really relevant. What is shown in Turner's painting is a large-scale disaster.

Shipwrecks in art and literature are announced by Falconer's poem *The Shipwreck*, published in 1762. See Byron's *Don Juan* Canto II for the most notable Romantic description, illustrated by Delacroix in *Le Naufrage de Don Juan*. Gericault's *The Raft of the Medusa* (1819) is another painting which is more than just a contemporary event. Looking again at Turner's painting with all these other parallels in mind, we can see here another great Romantic symbol. Man is at the mercy of natural forces, whatever his more civilized and superior self has to say. Perhaps his whole world is only a temporary phenomenon.

Through the Looking Glass

Yet, as so often in Shelley's poems, the *Ode to the West Wind* contains a counter-movement within itself. In our concentration upon the storm, we have omitted the strange passage in the third stanza:

> Thou who didst waken from his summer dreams
> The blue Mediterranean, where he lay,
> Lulled by the coil of his crystàlline streams,
>
> Beside a pumice isle in Baiae's bay,
> And saw in sleep old palaces and towers
> Quivering within the wave's intenser day,
>
> All overgrown with azure moss and flowers
> So sweet, the sense faints picturing them!

Compare the picture by Richard Wilson (108); we have already seen a general view of this Classical landscape in a Turner painting (74). Wilson shows us the reflected image of the grottoes and tower in the sea.

In Shelley's lines there is a similar reflected image, but also a reference to 'quivering'. There are many parallel passages in Romantic poetry, probably deriving from Wordsworth's *Elegiac Stanzas* (*Peele Castle*) where the image of the castle is reflected in a tranquil sea:

108 Richard Wilson, Torre delle Grotte, near Naples (c. 1753). Watercolour.

> It trembled, but it never passed away.

Elsewhere Wordsworth mentions

> . . . that uncertain heaven received
> Into the bosom of the steady lake . . .
> 'There was a boy . . .'

These may be explained as picturesque devices in Wordsworth, but the image haunts Shelley, and he is constantly referring to it (e.g. *The Witch of Atlas* ll. 513–5; *Ode to Liberty*, stanza vi; *Evening: Ponte al Mare, Pisa*). The surface of the water resembles Shelley's 'veil' which separates two worlds, one of 'shadows' and one of real things. But which is which? As a Platonist Shelley would know what to answer; the mirror image in the *Ode to the West Wind* may be a reminder of an eternal world, an 'intenser day' than ours.

On the other hand, the vision of the world below the sea in the concluding lines of the stanza is more difficult:

> . . . far below
> The sea-blooms and the oozy woods which wear
> The sapless foliage of the ocean, know
>
> Thy voice, and suddenly grow gray with fear,
> And tremble and despoil themselves: oh, hear!

We are drawn below the surface of the looking-glass world, into a place where there are trees and flowers far stranger than anything in our familiar surroundings. The passage can simply be taken as an account of the power of the storm, but if the storm is the 'collected lightning' of the Spirit of the Age, I think Shelley is trying to tell us that it will affect even the unconscious world which we can only reach in dreams.

Although it may be difficult to arrive at a satisfactory account of these passages, the fact remains that Shelley continually points towards another existence than our present state. At the end of *Adonais*, when the poet, in his 'Spirit's bark', is driven far from the shore by an even greater storm than that in the *Ode to the West Wind*, when

> The massy earth and spheréd skies are riven . . .

this is not to be taken as a premonition of personal catastrophe, but as the parting of the veil. He may be pursuing an illusion, but he beckons us to follow him into the abyss.

11 Descent into the Abyss

In ancient times no epic was complete without a descent into the Underworld; because Virgil (following Homer) had shown the terrors of the journey in *Aeneid* Book VI, he was naturally fitted to escort Dante over the threshold of Hell-Gate in the *Inferno* (109). In this section we try to reconstruct such a voyage into the interior of the earth in terms of English Romantic poetry; but whereas in Homer, Virgil or Dante there is some kind of literal belief to draw upon, our exploration must begin in a very dark wood indeed. Lost in a forest of symbols, we shall need to compare the experience of several of our poets, and to look for patterns which occur again and again.

109 William Blake, The inscription over Hell-Gate, *Illustrations to Dante's* Divine Comedy *no. 4 (1824–7). Chalk, pencil, pen and watercolour. Inscribed 'HELL Canto 3' and 'Lasciate ogni speranze voi che inentrate' over the arch: underneath the Italian is written 'Leave every Hope you who in Enter'.*

110 Joseph Wright of Derby, Virgil's Tomb *(1799). Oil.*

Keats' hero Endymion was compelled to make such a voyage, and shrank from it. In Book II of the poem he is led to the entrance to a cavern, near which a fountain rises—this linkage of symbols will recur. In fact, we have already seen such a picture in the first of the Voyage of Life paintings (45 i). From the depths of the cavern a voice is heard:

> . . . descend! He ne'er is crown'd
> With immortality, who fears to follow
> Where airy voices lead: so through the hollow,
> The silent mysteries of earth, descend!
>
> *Endymion* II, 211–4

With these words of encouragement, let us pursue our journey.

Entering upon the Quest

Joseph Wright's picture (110) is cool and clear. In fact, as we decided in considering previous works of this artist, we may feel that the surface meaning is all that is intended and that the painting is devoid of any hidden symbolism. It shows the reputed tomb of the poet Virgil. In the first century AD, in order to honour the dead, a later Roman poet, Silius Italicus, bought the land on which the tomb lay so that he could repair it. The painting shows him declaiming his verses before the tomb, which seems to be situated in a cave. The lighting is interesting: the moonlight is shining down from above, but there is another source of light, presumably a torch, below ground; notice the poet's shadow. The picture could also be seen as yet another example of an eighteenth century Classical landscape.

What is fascinating here is the link with later Romantic poems; this could be the scene of Shelley's *Hymn to Intellectual Beauty*, with the 'moonbeams' (1st and 3rd stanzas), clouds (1st and 4th stanzas), and the poet seeking from beyond the grave a solution to life's mysteries—

> No voice from some sublimer world hath ever
> To sage or poet these responses given . . .

Nevertheless, Shelley tells us:

> While yet a boy I sought for ghosts, and sped
> Through many a listening chamber, cave and ruin,
> And starlight wood, with fearful steps pursuing
> *Hopes of high talk with the departed dead.* (my italics)

The resemblances are very close, though Wright has none of Shelley's fevered ecstacy. The general symbols of moonlight, a cavern, and a poet in quest of knowledge are relevant to our present theme.

In this picture (111) John Martin illustrates an obscure Persian legend. The tiny figure in the corner is engaged in an impossible quest, and the towering mountains and crags are usually seen as 'the landscape of despair'. It is not clear whether we are above or below ground, so much do the rocks and precipices seem to hem us in.

111 John Martin, Sadak in Search of the Waters of Oblivion *(1812). Oil. Illustrates a story from James Ridley,* Tales of the Genii *(1762).*

This could be seen as an illustration to Endymion's search in Book II, after he has entered the cavern and journeys down towards the centre of the earth. *Hyperion*, too, is set in a mountainous underworld, and Book II 5–17, and 357–67 have been compared to this picture. Wider references than Keats need to be drawn from this chasm between towering rocks, and this roaring waterfall. At this point I would like to return to Wordsworth's *Prelude*.

The Chasm

After crossing the Alps (in Book VI) Wordsworth enters the narrow defile of the Simplon Pass. The landscape seems to be both hostile and alive with power and meaning:

> . . . Downwards we hurried fast,
> And, with the half-shaped road which we had missed,
> Entered a narrow chasm. The brook and road
> Were fellow-travellers in this gloomy strait,
> And with them did we journey several hours
> At a slow pace. The immeasurable height
> Of woods decaying, never to be decayed,
> The stationary blasts of waterfalls,
> And in the narrow rent at every turn
> Winds thwarting winds, bewildered and forlorn,
> The torrents shooting from the clear blue sky,
> The rocks that muttered close upon our ears,
> Black drizzling crags that spake by the way-side
> As if a voice were in them, the sick sight
> And giddy prospect of the raving stream,
> The unfettered clouds and region of the Heavens,
> Tumult and peace, the darkness and the light—
> Were all like workings of one mind, the features
> Of the same face, blossoms upon one tree;
> Characters of the great Apocalypse,
> The types and symbols of Eternity,
> Of first, and last, and midst, and without end.
> *The Prelude* 1850 Book VI, ll. 619–40

Notice 'the narrow rent', the mysterious 'voices', and the final comparison to the mind of God—I know this is to race over a number of questions, but all I want to do is to establish the presence of this kind of landscape in moments of vision.

Consider too the vision of 'a mighty Mind' which forms the beginning of the last book of *The Prelude*, the 'sea of mist' containing a chasm from which rises the noise of waters:

> The Moon stood naked in the Heavens, at height
> Immense above my head, and on the shore
> I found myself of a huge sea of mist,
> Which, meek and silent, rested at my feet:

A hundred hills their dusky backs upheaved
All over this still Ocean, and beyond,
Far, far beyond, the vapours shot themselves,
In headlands, tongues, and promontory shapes,
Into the Sea, the real Sea, that seem'd
To dwindle, and give up its majesty,
Usurp'd upon as far as sight could reach.
Meanwhile, the Moon look'd down upon this shew
In single glory, and we stood, the mist
Touching our very feet; and from the shore
At distance not the third part of a mile
Was a blue chasm; a fracture in the vapour,
A deep and gloomy breathing-place through which
Mounted the roar of waters, torrents, streams
Innumerable, roaring with one voice.
The universal spectacle throughout
Was shaped for admiration and delight,
Grand in itself alone, but in that breach
Through which the homeless voice of waters rose,
That dark deep thoroughfare had Nature lodg'd
The Soul, the Imagination of the whole.

The Prelude 1805 Book XIII, ll. 41–65

I grant that all this takes place on top of a mountain and is not part of an underworld journey. But notice the moon, and the description of the chasm as 'a deep and gloomy breathing-place', the voice from the depths, and the location of the soul and the imagination in 'that dark deep thoroughfare'.

Finally, and I hope conclusively, think of 'the deep Romantic chasm' in Coleridge's *Kubla Khan*, from which the fountain rises; it flings up the sacred river which later descends,

> Through caverns measureless to man
> Down to a sunless sea.

What I want to do now is to try to put all these images alongside one another, together with the evidence of the pictures.

The Abyss

The symbolism in these sequences of imagery can be interpreted in two ways, either in religious or in psychological terms. In many religious writings of the seventeenth and eighteenth centuries God is described as an 'abyss': for example, in the *Methodist Hymn Book*, Hymn No 42 (by John Wesley) begins:

> O God, Thou bottomless abyss . . .

If He is not Himself the abyss, then He is to be sought there. Consider this passage from Jacob Boehme, a seventeenth-century writer who greatly influenced the Romantics, whether at first or second hand:

> For as little as the life's own will can, in selfness and will turned away from God, stand still in Nature a moment from its working, unless it sink down beyond all Nature; so little can the divine speaking, in the life resigned to the ground, stand still from its working.
>
> For if the life stand still from its own will, it is in the abyss of Nature and creation, in the eternal divine utterance; and hence God speaks therein.

This is obscure but helpful; notice the imagery even if the theology is difficult. To reach God it is necessary to 'sink down'; and in the abyss there is a divine voice; thirdly, and this is often said in interpreting the Wordsworth and Coleridge passages, the abyss is the source of creativity—or *potential* creativity.

It is therefore quite possible to interpret all the symbolism in a non-religious way; in this case we would say that it refers to the location of 'the creative imagination' which is in some sense *below* normal mental activity. We might say today that these passages discuss the relation between the conscious and the sub-conscious mind. The word 'sub-conscious' was not then in the language. Such an interpretation of the passages cited above would see the narrow cleft or chasm as a link between the conscious world of reason, light and colour, and a deeper level of the mind, irrational, dark and obscure. Therefore, in these Romantic contexts, to 'descend into the underworld' is to plunge into the depths of the mind, and to try to listen to its strange and difficult utterances. Yet here too are the springs of creativity, the fountain of life and the sacred river, the sources of knowledge and power.

The Labyrinth

In discussing this symbolism I have simplified the strenuous journey that is implied in the quest; physical effort precedes both the Wordsworth passages. In Classical stories we find a clear account of the dangers; the Sibyl at Cumae, like the priestess at Delphi, was thought to be inspired by vapours rising from the depths of a chasm or cleft in the earth; to reach the Sibyl Aeneas has to enter a labyrinth. We have already noticed that Shelley referred to this when describing the human mind as a 'wilderness' which the Wanderer had to traverse (p. 64); look again at the front endpaper. According to Thomas De Quincey, Coleridge also saw the mind as a labyrinth; he loved to examine the nightmare-like prison sequence by Piranesi, the *Carceri d' Invenzione*, of which one plate is

reproduced here (112). In his *Confessions of an English Opium-Eater* De Quincey tells us that Coleridge used these pictures as a stimulant to the imagination. They are of course a kind of architectural fantasy, and therefore very close to the visions allegedly seen by both writers in their opium dreams. According to De Quincey, the various bridges and staircases in Piranesi's Prisons appear to lead somewhere, but in fact there is no way out; he saw one figure on all the staircases:

> Many years ago, when I was looking over Piranesi's 'Antiquities of Rome', Coleridge, then standing by, described to me a set of plates from that artist, called his 'Dreams,' and which record the scenery of his own visions during the delirium of a fever. Some of these (I describe only from memory of Coleridge's account) represented vast Gothic halls; on the floor of which stood mighty engines and machinery, wheels, cables, catapults, &c., expressive of enormous power put forth, or resistance overcome. Creeping along the sides of the walls, you perceived a staircase; and upon this, groping his way upwards, was Piranesi himself. Follow the stairs a little farther, and you perceive them reaching an abrupt termination, without any balustrade, and allowing no step onwards to him who should reach the extremity, except into the depths below. Whatever is to become of poor Piranesi, at least you suppose that his labours must now in some way terminate. But raise your eyes, and behold a second flight of stairs still higher, on which again Piranesi is perceived, by this time standing on the very brink of the abyss. Once again elevate your eye, and a still more aerial flight of stairs is descried; and there, again, is the delirious Piranesi, busy on his aspiring labours: and so on, until the unfinished stairs and the hopeless Piranesi both are lost in the upper gloom of the hall.

Keats, too, in a letter of 3 May 1818, used the figure of the labyrinth to explain the quest for knowledge to ease 'the burden of the mystery':

> you seem . . . to have been going through with a more painful and acute zest the same labyrinth that I have. . . .

He describes the 'geography' more clearly a few pages later:

> I compare human life to a large Mansion of Many Apartments, two of which I can only describe, the doors of the rest being as yet shut upon me. The first we step into we call the infant or thoughtless Chamber, in which we remain as long as we do not think. We remain there a long while, and not withstanding the doors of the second Chamber remain wide open, showing a bright appearance, we care not to hasten to it; but are at length imperceptibly impelled by the awakening of the thinking principle within us—we no sooner get into the second Chamber, which I shall call the Chamber of Maiden-Thought, than we become intoxicated with the light and the atmosphere, we see nothing but pleasant wonders, and think of delaying there for ever in delight. However among the effects this breathing is father of is that tremendous one of sharpening one's vision into the heart and nature of Man—of convincing one's nerves that the world is full of Misery and Heartbreak, Pain, Sickness and oppression—whereby this Chamber of Maiden Thought becomes gradually darken'd and at the same time on all sides of it many doors are set open—but all dark—all leading to dark passages. We see not the ballance of good and evil. We are in a Mist. *We* are now in that state—We feel the 'burden of the Mystery'. To this point was Wordsworth come, as far as I can conceive when he wrote 'Tintern Abbey' and it seems to me that his Genius is explorative of those dark Passages.

Keats seems to have recurred to this vision in the introduction to *The Fall of Hyperion*, where the poet finds himself in a cavern like a cathedral. But this we shall need to discuss later. Meanwhile we too must explore 'the dark passages' of the labyrinth; what is in them may give us pause to think.

The Monsters of the Deep

(i) The Doppelgänger

In a famous passage in *Prometheus Unbound* Shelley sets out a strange teaching about 'the two worlds of life and death':

> Ere Babylon was dust
> The Magus Zoroaster, my dead child,
> Met his own image walking in the garden.
> That apparition, sole of men, he saw.
> For know there are two worlds of life and death:
> One that which thou beholdest; but the other
> Is underneath the grave, where do inhabit
> The shadows of all forms that think and live
> Till death unite them and they part no more;
>
> *Prometheus Unbound* Act I 191–9

113 Dante Gabriel Rossetti, How they met themselves (1851–60) Pen and ink drawing.

114 George Stubbs, Horse frightened by a lion *(1770). Oil.*

Rossetti's drawing, *How they met themselves* (113), shows a pair of lovers who meet with their doubles in a wood at twilight. I have not been able to find another treatment of this theme strictly within the Romantic period, and though up to now I have tried to exclude late nineteenth-century artists it is only fair to point out how much the Pre-Raphaelites in particular were indebted to the Romantic poets. One can see this drawing simply as a 'bogie', to quote Rossetti, but it does hint at something more than the German legend it professes to illustrate. Like the Brocken spectre (33) it can lead us to speculate about the reason for such a phenomenon; even if our rational common sense confines it to the world of dreams. Traditionally, such a meeting was a warning of the approach of death; Shelley, we are told by Thomas Medwin, met his own image at Casa Magni—it spoke to him, saying 'How long do you mean to be content?' De Quincey, too, in an astonishing passage of the *Confessions*, saw himself appear at a window in the market-place at Altrincham.

(ii) Lions and Tigers

Stubbs' picture of a *Horse frightened by a lion* (114) could, I suppose, be understood at a literal level as yet another study of the horse by a painter who had made his name with his accurate delineation of the anatomy of the animal, and with paintings of famous race-horses. This, however, will hardly do.

The face of the lion appears dramatically from the darkness, almost as if it were unrelated to a body; the landscape too, is strange; there is a ravine or rocky defile, and to the left a stream—exactly the symbolic background which we have been learning to read. The horse is considered to be a rational creature above all others—think of the Houyhnhnms in Book IV of *Gulliver's Travels*; the picture could be interpreted as showing how reasonable eighteenth-century intelligence is unable to cope with the strange creatures of the Romantic imagination.

We might compare Wordsworth, in Paris shortly after the September Massacres in 1792, and unable to sleep:

> The place, all hushed and silent as it was,
> Appeared unfit for the repose of night,
> Defenceless as a wood where tigers roam.
> *The Prelude* 1850 Book X, ll. 91–3

Blake, of course, accepts the Tiger (115) into his world of Experience: at first sight the creature in the illustration seems almost harmless. But the questions posed in the poem are disconcerting, to say the least. There are Promethean references, too, in the second stanza. The crucial question comes in the last stanza but one:

> Did he who made the Lamb make thee?

115 *William Blake*, The Tyger, *Plate 42 of* Songs of Experience *(1794). Etching with coloured washes. The picture of the tiger varies from the fierce to the cat-like in different versions.*

If we could solve this riddle—called by one editor, 'The riddle of the Universe'—then the Romantic quest would seem to have some end in sight.

'When the stars threw down their spears' is a reference to the Book of Job, which is a meditation upon the place of evil and suffering in human existence, and can be considered as one attempt to solve what Keats and Wordsworth meant by 'the burden of the mystery'. The Book of Job was illustrated by Blake in the last years of his life, though it is known that he had been considering such a project for many years. Blake's illustrations contain an implicit commentary upon the Bible story, and several interpretations have been offered. At the climax of the book 'The Lord answers Job out of the whirlwind', and gives examples of his creative power: 'Behold now Behemoth which I made with thee' (116). According

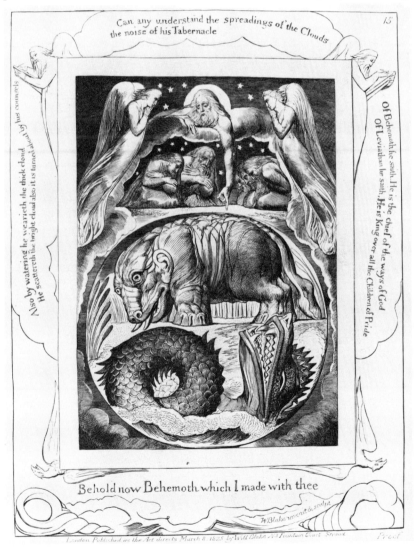

116 William Blake, Behemoth and Leviathan, *Plate 15 from* Illustrations of the Book of Job *(1825). Engraving. The text at the bottom is Job 40 v. 15; the other texts are a collage of references in no particular order though they are all from Job 36–41.*

to the orthodox interpretation these huge and uncontrollable creatures show the utter incomprehensibility of the Creator; we cannot understand why such monsters exist, but at least they show the human observer that he is not in a rational universe. Blake gives Behemoth—presumably the hippopotamus—a human ear; his stillness is in contradiction to the Leviathan—a crocodile or sea-monster—who is lashing the waters. These two monsters relate to one another within a circle. The problem is to decide on the meaning of the circle, which may be related to the sphere of material creation (see *The Ancient of Days* (11)): one commentator, S. Foster Damon, calls it the sphere of the subconscious, 'the unredeemed portion of the psyche'. Job, his wife, and his three friends are at the top of the picture, looking down; God points across them to the creatures in the circle, as if urging them to take notice of these creatures, to relate to them in some way.

To sum up, these violent and potentially aggressive monsters which inhabit the depths, whether seen as lions, tigers or fabulous beasts, show us—on the two levels of meaning already suggested for the abyss— firstly, the mysterious ways of God, and his creation of irrational and perhaps evil beings in what one would like to be an orderly world; secondly, they are symbols of equally menacing and strange elements within the human mind. These the poet must at least recognize and face, even if he cannot control or understand. If he could trust them, he might find, as Blake said, that 'The Tigers of wrath are wiser than the horses of instruction'.

117 Henry Fuseli, Macbeth and the Armed Head *(c. 1778–80). Pen and ink.*

(iii) Demogorgon

This picture by Fuseli (117) is an illustration to Shakespeare's *Macbeth*. To remind you of the story, a tyrant and a murderer seeks reassurance from the powers of darkness; the witches summon up a series of visions; one of them is an armed head. To use our terminology, Fuseli shows the apparition rising from the abyss. Similarly, in *Prometheus Unbound*, the tyrant Jupiter is ultimately confronted and dethroned by a mysterious and violent power, Demogorgon. This strange deity rises from the abyss, where we are assured, it has been waiting since the beginning of time for its hour. Demogorgon is a difficult symbol to interpret; he has been described as Necessity, i.e. historical determinism, the inevitable changing of society by revolution and war. Nevertheless, he represents some kind of retributive Justice. Jupiter says:

> Awful shape, what art thou? Speak.

Demogorgon replies:

> Eternity. Demand no direr name.
> Descend and follow me down the abyss. . . .

He carries Jupiter away, leading to the enigmatic conclusion when 'conquest is dragged captive through the deep'. The problem is to decide whether this is really a beneficent power at all, or simply a personification of the Last Judgement which cannot be avoided. (Remember how Kubla Khan, secure in his pleasure dome, heard from the depths 'ancestral voices prophesying war'.) Traditionally, Demogorgon lived at the bottom of a volcano; like the West Wind, he is more of a destroyer than preserver. We have yet another example of salvation by catastrophe.

Visions of Cosmic Disaster

While it is easy to ridicule John Martin's pictures, with their 'columns a mile high' and 'courtyards six miles long', we need to account for their popularity in their day. Martin is apparently offering religious instruction, and showing the power of the Lord—against which nothing human can stand. He confronts a seemingly settled establishment with unexpected disaster, offering a view of history which might well haunt the back of the mind during a revolutionary period. As Babylon had fallen (118), so might London. In an age when the Bible was literally believed by most people, one could still encounter representatives of apocalyptic sects who announced the impending Day of Judgement. And so John Martin offered pictures of *The Great Day of His Wrath* and *The Deluge* (119).

The Deluge continues the theme of Turner's *The Shipwreck*, destruction by water. Notice in Martin's picture how tiny the Ark appears, as if it is regrettable than any form of salvation should be available. (It is on top of a mountain near the sun.) Remember that even 'atheists' like Shelley believed that the Deluge in the Bible had happened at a definite time in the past; as we shall see, its effects could still be noticed, according to the teachings of geologists.

John Martin illustrates a view of world history which would appear to make good sense to quite reasonable people at the time. History was simply a series of catastrophes, showing the wrath of God—or, if you were Shelley, the power of Demogorgon. We can begin to see why so much contemporary painting shows scenes of disaster, whether by sea or land. It is John Martin's sense of scale that makes him the foremost painter of these visions from the abyss.

Though there are possible influences of John Martin upon Keats—Dr Ian Jack, in his *Keats and the Mirror of Art*, suggests that *The Fall of Babylon* is close to the description of Hyperion's palace, which

Glared a blood-red through all its thousand courts.

John Martin, The
of Babylon *(1819)*.

The most obvious parallels to these pictures are to be found in the work of Shelley. There are constant exaggerations of the scale and size of disaster in *The Revolt of Islam* and in *Hellas*; even the comparatively sober *Triumph of Life* has a '. . . million with fierce song and maniac dance Raging around . . .' a chariot like a Juggernaut. Remember, too, 'the pestilence-stricken multitudes' who briefly appear in the *Ode to the West Wind*. Shelley relies too much upon catastrophe to resolve his difficulties, so that the endings of many poems give no adequate answer to the problems posed. (For example, the 'phantom' in *England in 1819*, or 'Spring' at the end of the *West Wind*.) We are led to expect the communication of some vital information, and a violent explosion is no real answer to 'the riddle of the Universe'.

The Sphinx

John Martin, The
ge *(1828)*. *Mezzotint.*
in provided a
hlet containing 37
from Byron's Heaven
Earth. The sun, moon
comet are in
nction—providing a
ific reason for the high
The ark is in the
e.

Our journey into the abyss has come to a halt; before we begin the ascent let us recapitulate what has been achieved. This remarkable picture by Ingres (120) illustrates the legend of Oedipus and the Sphinx; in the Greek story, the Sphinx asked a riddle and those who could not solve it were destroyed—notice the bones. Only Oedipus realizes that the answer is 'Man' and so delivers the city of Thebes from the monster.

But notice, too, in this painting, how all the symbolic references of the quest into the abyss are present. First, the narrow cleft or chasm in the rocks; secondly, in the half-light, the hero encounters the dangerous and

120 Ingres, Oedipus and the Sphinx *(1808). Oil.*

ambiguous monster*; thirdly, the quest for secret knowledge—in this case does it not look as if Oedipus is asking the questions? Yet we end with a riddle. To quote the last chorus of Shelley's *Hellas:*

> Although a subtler Sphinx renew
> Riddles of death Thebes never knew . . .

We have come a long way from Joseph Wright's picture (110), yet notice how much of the same symbolic landscape is present.

* Yeats' 'sphinx with woman breast and lion paw' is derived from this picture.

12 The Secrets of an Elder Day

On his return from the centre of the earth, as Endymion wandered through the depths of the sea, he encountered

> Old rusted anchors, helmets, breast-plates large
> Of gone sea-warriors; brazen beaks and targe;
> Rudders that for a hundred years had lost
> The sway of human hand; gold vase emboss'd
> With long-forgotten story, and wherein
> No reveller had ever dipp'd a chin
> But those of Saturn's vintage; mouldering scrolls,
> Writ in the tongue of heaven, by those souls
> Who first were on the earth; and sculptures rude
> In ponderous stone, developing the mood
> Of ancient Nox;—then skeletons of man,
> Of beast, behemoth, and leviathan,
> And elephant, and eagle, and huge jaw
> Of nameless monster. A cold leaden awe
> These secrets struck into him . . .
>
> *Endymion* III, 123 ff.

What exactly are 'these secrets'? Let us leave aside the human remains for the moment and start at the bottom of the list. 'Behemoth and leviathan' we have already met—but surely these are fabulous beasts? Nevertheless the passage has an odd ring of truth about it, however muddled the archaeology and geology may appear to our present thinking. Though the age saw the beginnings of scientific geology, there was no conflict with religion in the minds of many of its practitioners. In 1819 Professor Buckland announced in his inaugural lecture at Oxford: 'The grand fact of an universal deluge at no very remote period is proved on grounds so decisive and incontrovertible, that had we never heard of such an event from Scripture or any other Authority, Geology of itself must have called in the assistance of some such catastrophe to explain the phenomena of diluvial action.'

121 Frontispiece of James Parkinson, Organic Remains of a Former World *(1804–11) Vol 1*.

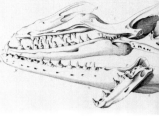

122 Jaw of large fossil animal from Maastricht, *from James Parkinson,* Organic Remains of a Former World *(1804–11) Vol 3 Plate XIX*.

The Antediluvian World

If you examine the frontispiece to James Parkinson's *Organic Remains of a Former World: An Examination of the Mineralised Remains of the Vegetables and Animals of the Antediluvian World* (121) you can see the Ark in the distance, resting on a mountain top, with the rainbow alongside. In the foreground are to be seen shattered rocks emerging from the sea, with fossils strangely prominent. A later plate (122) shows the jaw of a 'nameless monster'. This could also be a relic of Leviathan; looking back at Blake's picture (116) one can see that his Leviathan has a distinctly saurian appearance. I think it is also possible that Blake's Behemoth is based upon a picture of a mammoth; in 1806 a specimen had been discovered in Siberia, preserved in a deep-frozen state in the ice, except for its trunk which had been eaten by dogs.

All these remains had to related to the accepted history of the Earth. As Parkinson's frontispiece suggests, fossils are the organic remains of an earlier epoch; the former world had been totally destroyed by the Flood. The French scientist, Georges Cuvier (1769–1832), in trying to explain stratification, had suggested that the Biblical Flood was only the latest of many catastrophes which the Earth had suffered:

Numberless living beings have been the victims of these catastrophes; some have been destroyed by sudden inundations; others have been laid dry in consequence of the bottom of the seas being instantaneously elevated. Their races even have become extinct, and have left no memorial of them except some small fragments which the naturalist can scarcely recognise. . . .

Theory of the Earth, translated by Robert Kerr 1813

Primal Catastrophe

Geologists of this school were known as Catastrophists. Byron and Shelley believed what Cuvier taught. We also know that Shelley had read Parkinson; he expounds a similar view of Earth history in *Prometheus Unbound*: the Spirit of the Earth projects 'beams' of a penetrating light into the 'dark soil, and as they pierce and pass/Make bare the secrets. . . .'

> The beams flash on
> And make appear the melancholy ruins
> Of cancelled cycles; anchors, beaks of ships;
> Planks turned to marble; quivers, helms, and spears,
> And gorgon-headed targes, and the wheels
> Of scythèd chariots, and the emblazonry
> Of trophies, standards, and armorial beasts,
> Round which death laughed, sepulchred emblems
> Of dead destruction, ruin within ruin!
> The wrecks beside of many a city vast,
> Whose population which the earth grew over
> Was mortal, but not human; see, they lie,
> Their monstrous works, and uncouth skeletons,
> Their statues, homes and fanes; prodigious shapes
> Huddled in gray annihilation, split,
> Jammed in the hard, black deep; and over these,
> The anatomies of unknown wingèd things,
> And fishes which were isles of living scale,
> And serpents, bony chains, twisted around
> The iron crags, or within heaps of dust
> To which the tortuous strength of their last pangs
> Had crushed the iron crags; and over these
> The jaggèd alligator, and the might
> Of earth-convulsing behemoth, which once
> Were monarch beasts, and on the slimy shores,
> And weed-overgrown continents of earth,
> Increased and multiplied like summer worms
> On an abandoned corpse, till the blue globe
> Wrapped deluge round it like a cloak, and they
> Yelled, gasped, and were abolished; or some God
> Whose throne was in a comet, passed, and cried,
> 'Be not!' And like my words they were no more.

Prometheus Unbound IV, ll. 287–318

Notice 'the isles of living scale' (presumably Leviathan) and Behemoth once again; probably the passage is imitated from Keats. The comet at the end is spectacular, and was one way of accounting for the violent upheavals; comets were thought to be solid objects, and therefore capable of exerting immense forces. In Buffon's picture (123) God, or 'some God' as in Shelley, looks on while a comet strikes the sun, producing gaseous exhalations which will cool into the Solar System; it would therefore be a comparatively minor matter for a passing comet to attract the waters of the Earth to rise as high as the mountain tops—an explanation of the Deluge suggested by Sir Humphry Davy— or to produce unexpected and catastrophic earthquakes. Look again at the Martin picture (119), and consider it as illustrating a scientific rather than Biblical account of History.

All this may seem a long way from the Medieval and Renaissance world-picture of an ordered Universe, which had lingered within the eighteenth-century ideas of the Great Architect and his careful constructions (11, 12). Nor could one continue to imagine a Chain of Being in which all creatures found a useful and rightful place in the scheme of Nature. On our own planet alone it seemed that a series of separate creations had taken place and then been wiped out in a series of catastrophes, while out in the wider Universe Shelley could only see that

123 Catastrophic Origin of the Solar System, *Plate from Buffon* Histoire Naturelle, *edition of 1769–72.*

> Worlds on worlds are rolling ever
> From creation to decay,
> Like the bubbles on a river
> Sparkling, bursting, borne away.
> *Hellas* ll. 197–200

Was it possible that within human history too there had been a series of 'cancelled cycles'? The Bible and other mythologies seemed to indicate that the last major cycle had been completed by the Flood; and though human remains were not usually thought to antedate this point in time, odd things which turned up seemed inexplicable in the light of conventional accounts of history, such as walls which appeared to have been constructed by giants. As Shelley and Keats state in their poems, these might be relics of antediluvian civilizations, whether described as 'pre-Adamite' or 'those of Saturn's vintage'; and after all, even within recorded history it was possible to observe the operations of a wheel of Time.

The Course of Empire

The Course of Empire (124, i–v) is another series of paintings by Thomas Cole. Though they date from the 1830s, this hardly matters since they confirm the continuity of the idea throughout the Romantic Period.

In style they resemble the dioramas still to be seen in many museums. In each picture we see the same place—a valley—but it is surveyed from five different viewpoints in order to avoid monotony. A single detail dominates: the same towering cliff with a boulder at its peak can be discerned in all the scenes, and used as a point of reference.

124 Thomas Cole, The Course of Empire (1836). Oil. A series of five pictures, each approximately 100 cm × 160 cm, except the middle one, which is 130 cm × 193 cm.

AVAGE STATE—The valley is filled
th trees, a mist hangs in the air—it
early morning in Spring. Notice
t the brook is unbridged. Savages
 seen hunting for their food; they
 equipped with bows and spears,
d are capable of building wigwams
d small rowing-boats.

ARCADIAN STATE—This is the
lden Age. On a June morning we
serve the agricultural activities of a
riarchal society—sheep-farming
d ploughing. A simple bridge
sses the brook; a small town has
wn up and sailing boats are in use.
tice the Euclid-figure busy with
ometry, and the Stonehenge temple
sumably served by Druids.

iii CONSUMMATION OF EMPIRE—The Classical Age. It is noon on a hot August day. The vices of luxury are already becoming apparent. (In the cyclical theory decline usually stems from moral laxity.)

iv DESTRUCTION OF EMPIRE—Goths and Vandals do their work on an Autumn evening.

v DESOLATION—shows only ruins; it is winter and the time is midnight. The lonely pillar is in fact taken from the actual column in Rome which is referred to by Byron.

The whole series, says Cole, illustrates 'how nations have risen from the savage state to that of power and glory and become extinct.' The process is heavily underlined by the seasonal changes* in the paintings and the sequence of time from early morning to midnight. We can also see more clearly how Turner's earlier but more famous paintings, *Dido Building Carthage, or the Rise of the Carthaginian Empire* and *The Decline of the Carthaginian Empire* would be interpreted. Carthage was a sea-power which lived by trade; but it could not avoid its fate. Britain, similarly a sea-power, and even though apparently victorious over France—a land-based power like Rome, with Roman Imperial associations encouraged by Napoleon—could not survive for ever at the high crest of its apparent supremacy.

The series also helps us to understand the late eighteenth-century associations of the word 'Revolution'. We normally use this word in contexts which imply a violent, and possibly unexpected, overthrow of a government. But if History proceeds in a predetermined cycle then a revolution is simply the inevitable turning of the wheel, and may be a gradual process. One of Shelley's most-used source-books was Volney's *Ruins*, subtitled *A Survey of the Revolutions of Empires*. The action—such of it as is of this world—takes place amid the ruins of Palmyra in the Syrian Desert. Volney, a wanderer and a student of history, finds himself benighted in this deserted city. A spectre appears, releases him from his corporeal frame, and conveys him into the uppermost regions of the atmosphere. From this elevated viewpoint he learns the unavoidable fate of human societies: ruination and decay. (Compare *Queen Mab* II, 110.) There is, however, the hope that in an enlightened state far to the West a new kind of revolution may take place in the name of Liberty, Equality and Justice which will release men from the usual downward turning of the wheel. It comes as a shock to look at the front of the book and to find that Volney wrote all this in 1784, if not before. (He died in 1820, desiring that DÉSILLUSIONNÉ should be inscribed on his tomb.)

Shelley, however much we may think of him as the apostle of Godwin, Progress and Perfectibility, was haunted by the cyclical vision of History. At the end of *Hellas*, written in 1821, his fears seem to be momentarily overcome in the famous chorus beginning

> The world's great age begins anew,
> The golden years return . . .

The 'Revolutions of Empires' become trivial as they are subsumed in a greater cycle. The whole of the time-process is seen as circular, and all past events will be re-enacted as the Great Wheel of History turns back to the beginning. 'Saturn and Love their long repose/Shall burst. . . .'—and so we shall retrieve innocence and recapture the freshness of the Golden

*A metaphor also present in 'If Winter comes, can Spring be far behind?'

Age. But then Shelley remembers that 'hate and death' must also return in their due place in the cycle, leading to the hopeless conclusion to the poem:

> The world is weary of the past,
> Oh, might it die or rest at last!

125 John Martin, The Sea Dragons as they lived. *Mezzotint. Frontispiece to Thomas Hawkins,* The Book of the Great Sea Dragons: Ichthyosauri and Plesiosauri *(1840).*

The Theory of Development

There was of course another way of interpreting the evidence of 'the secrets' and making them conform to some kind of order. Could each cycle, whether of animal or human history, have been superseded by a higher form of life or polity? This is a late picture (125), though it is a clear statement of the problem posed by geological discoveries; remember that the ichthyosaurus had been unearthed by Mary Anning at Lyme Regis in 1811, and may be the reference in Shelley's 'isles of living scale'. Other saurians would soon make their appearance. Apart from challenging Biblical chronology, they upset many assumptions about the wisdom and benevolence of God. Their horrific appearance, and the aggressive way of life they were assumed to have led, cried out against the prevailing ideology; having allowed them their brutish lives, what was the purpose of their extinction? But if life had developed from lower to higher forms, what did this imply about human beings and human society? Crude theories of development had been in circulation in the 1790s, but they were not welcome at that time, for obvious political reasons. In 1819—which we have already noted as a key year in our interpretation of the period—Dr Lawrence proposed a theory of biological 'Progress' in his book *The Natural History of Man*; he was forced to withdraw his views. 'What is to become of the morals of the populace,' said E.W. Grinfield, one of his opponents, 'if they should once adopt your opinions?'

Keats' *Hyperion* is about the events which take place at the end of a cycle, the Saturnian, and during the beginning of a new age. The poem

168

has often been understood to refer to political change, which is a reflection of biological processes. In order to comprehend this, it is necessary for Apollo to be given the secret knowledge of 'creatings and destroyings' so that he may understand the past. The submerged Titans, in many ways similar in their build and behaviour to Martin's 'sea dragons', are unable to accept the words of Oceanus, who advises them to submit:

> "Now comes the pain of truth, to whom 'tis pain;
> "O folly! for to bear all naked truths,
> "And to envisage circumstance, all calm.
> "That is the top of sovereignty. Mark well!
> "As Heaven and Earth are fairer, fairer far
> "Than Chaos and blank Darkness, though once chiefs;
> "And as we show beyond that Heaven and Earth
> "In form and shape compact and beautiful,
> "In will, in action free, companionship,
> "And thousand other signs of purer life;
> "So on our heels a fresh perfection treads,
> "A power more strong in beauty, born of us
> "And fated to excel us, as we pass
> "In glory that old Darkness: nor are we
> "Thereby more conquer'd, than by us the rule
> "Of shapeless Chaos. Say, doth the dull soil
> "Quarrel with the proud forests it hath fed,
> "And feedeth still, more comely than itself?
> "Can it deny the chiefdom of green groves?
> "Or shall the tree be envious of the dove
> "Because it cooeth, and hath snowy wings
> "To wander wherewithal and find its joys?
> "We are such forest-trees, and our fair boughs
> "Have bred forth, not pale solitary doves,
> "But eagles golden-feather'd, who do tower
> "Above us in their beauty, and must reign
> "In right thereof; for 'tis the eternal law
> "That first in beauty should be first in might . . .
>
> *Hyperion* II, ll. 202–229

It is Keats alone who is able to solve the riddles of the abyss, and to bring the secrets of the elder day to light. He offers an escape from catastrophism, and from the wheel of history, and proposes a relationship between Man and the other creatures of the earth. He shows a respect for Nature and its processes, however strange and monstrous a form they seem to take. Like Coleridge's Mariner, he blesses the water-snakes; though we needn't go so far as to suggest that Keats had stumbled on natural selection — a possible interpretation of 'first in beauty should be first in might' — we can see the beginning here of a new poetry of order and calm, a new Chain of Being stretching backwards into Time, in which even the 'sea dragons' could find a place.

13 Finale: Poetry and the Poet

From this age of turmoil and speculation we see a new ideal of poetry emerging. In the first place, it was no longer sufficient to regard poetry merely as an attribute of urban civilized man and as a vehicle for social comment; one could only begin to understand poetry by tracing it back to its natural origins; the poet should try to recapture the place he held in primitive society.

The Natural Origin of the Arts

If we examine J. M. Gandy's drawing of *Architecture: its natural model* (126) we can see the origins of a more visually interesting art than poetry. Once again we see the world after the Deluge! To quote Sir John Summerson's description:

126 Joseph Michael Gandy, Architecture: its natural model *(1838). Watercolour.*

The painting represents a wild, mountainous, almost Arctic scene—the world after the subsidence of the flood. A careful survey of the more distant mountains reveals Noah's Ark, stranded high on the very peak of Ararat. In the centre of the composition is a valley with a river, flowing towards the spectator, while all around are natural phenomena suggesting architectural forms. There is a 'Fingal's Cave'—nature's Gothic nave; there are alps, icebergs, glaciers, spire-like rocks, and a 'natural' bridge; proto-architectural forms emerge among the rocks and hills, and the materials for a primitive architecture abound. Beavers, bees and white ants are at work and in the foreground an orang-outang has constructed a hut in the entry of which his mate and offspring are visible. A palm tree, with a vine climbing up its trunk, suggests types of ornament; and the skeleton of a primitive reptile shows the serrated jaws which are the reputed origin of the saw ... Gandy's thought has receded beyond architecture and beyond archaeology into a semi-biblical anthropology.

from *Heavenly Mansions* New York (1963)

In *The Defence of Poetry*, to which I shall often refer in this section, Shelley proposes a similar origin for poetry: 'In the youth of the world, men dance and sing and imitate natural objects, observing in these actions, as in all others, a certain rhythm or order. . . . In the infancy of society every author is necessarily a poet, because language itself is poetry'.

The Song of Birds

The obvious natural analogue to poetry is birdsong; in particular, the song of the skylark is an ageless comparison for the *effortless flow* of lyric poetry. Our poets took good care to cultivate an impression of spontaneity, so that Wordsworth and Shelley both compare the skylark to the poet. In his poem of that name, Shelley praises its 'unpremeditated art', and also brings in 'cloud' references which link this symbol to the chain of 'skiey imagery' already discussed. The Skylark, its song audible even when it is soaring too high to be seen, is the image of Sublimity, and of the dash and verve of Romantic aspiration. Palmer's etching (127) shows the lark at dawn; the accompanying text is from Milton's *L'Allegro*.

7 *Samuel Palmer*, The ylark. *Etching 1850), state V. Related a watercolour of 1831–2.*

> To hear the lark begin his flight
> And singing startle the dull night,
> From his watch-tower in the skies
> Till the dappled dawn doth rise. . . .

Watch-towers will be discussed later. Meanwhile one should perhaps note that the cuckoo, heard far off (Wordsworth), the wild swan, dying (Shelley), and many other birds make a significant appearance in English Romantic poetry*: and, as one might expect, Clare scores over all the others in the range and accuracy of his observations. We are more concerned with the symbolic meaning of these references, if any; the

*There are some interesting facts about the poets' observations in *The Shell Book of Birds* by James Fisher (pp.188-194).

nightingale, which is a major reference in poems by Coleridge and Keats, is also an image in the *Defence*: 'A poet is a nightingale, who sits in darkness and sings'. This 'darkness' adds another, more mysterious dimension.

The Bard

The poets of 'the infancy of society' were also mysterious figures. In the late eighteenth century English poetry is haunted by bards. Most of them derive from a poem called *The Bard*, a Pindaric Ode by Thomas Gray, which was illustrated in a well-known painting by John Martin. More useful for our purpose is this picture of *The Bard* by Thomas Jones (128), which provides a link to Stonehenge, the Druids, and the mysterious British past. Whatever later research may have done to undermine the importance of the Druids, our poets accepted all the legends about them, and Wordsworth imagined a scene like this while he was crossing Salisbury Plain (*The Prelude* 1850 XIII, ll. 313 ff). The Druid Arch appears in many of Blake's illustrations of his own poetry; and *Songs of Experience* begins with a request to 'Hear the voice of the Bard'—a figure who combines the roles of Druid and Old Testament Prophet. Bard and Druid were both thought of as having high authority in society; see again Shelley's *Defence*: 'Poets . . . were called, in the earlier epochs of the world, legislators, or prophets. . . .'

The Aeolian Harp

In the previous picture the bard was clutching a harp, or lyre, the ancient symbol for poetry. In the Romantic Age this symbolism again became common, even on chairbacks. But a special significance was attached to the Aeolian or wind-harp (129). The principle behind this had been known in ancient times, and is referred to in one of the Hymns attributed to Homer. In the middle of the eighteenth century the Aeolian Harp became a popular 'toy'. It could be made to play by hanging it in a window or even on a tree, and its effect can be heard by anyone today who stands near overhead telephone wires in a storm. Technical details can be discovered from Grove's *Dictionary of Music;* the picture (130) shows how an Aeolian Harp was constructed in the eighteenth century.

The Wind Harp entered English literature in James Thomson's *Castle of Indolence* (1748). Thereafter nearly every poet seems to mention it or refer to it, until the end of the Romantic period. In Wordsworth the soul has 'Aeolian visitations'; Coleridge wrote a poem called *The Aeolian Harp*, which describes the gentler moods of the instrument—he concludes by speculating

128 Thomas Jones, The
Bard *(1774)*. Oil. Notice
the henge in the
background.

129 Detail from J. M. W.
Turner, Thomson's
Aeolian Harp *(1809)*. The
wind-harp was the subject
of an Ode by Thomson,
and also featured in The
Castle of Indolence.

130 Aeolian Harp (c.
1800). Aeolus was the god
of the winds.

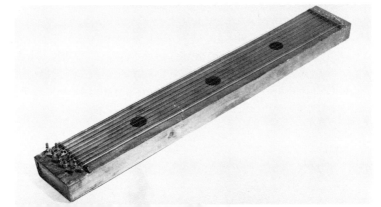

> And what if all of animated nature
> Be but organic Harps diversely framed,
> That tremble into thought, as o'er them sweeps
> Plastic and vast, one intellectual breeze,
> At once the Soul of each, and God of all?

But this rather vague pantheism is not the usual meaning which the Harp invokes. In a very early poem by Wordsworth — *The Vale of Esthwaite* — a wandering minstrel finds that a Phantom 'smites the wire' of the harp on his back; in Coleridge's *Dejection* the Aeolian 'lute' screams in the storm; and Shelley requests the West Wind to

> Make me thy lyre, even as the forest is.

The symbolism becomes clearer and adds up to a theory of poetry: the Harp *is* the Poet, who is blown and buffeted by the Wind of Inspiration. The poetry produced in this way is beyond the control of the conscious mind; it is oracular, and may appear in disconnected fragments.

In fact we know that most of our poets, even Shelley, worked away at draft upon draft of their poems, but the important point to notice is that they did not choose to parade this fact; rather the reverse, so that the long note by Coleridge which accompanies *Kubla Khan* insists that the poem is a fragment which came to the poet in a dream. It is quite possible that one day a manuscript will turn up to disprove Coleridge's assertion, but this will not detract from the historical importance of the theory of inspiration.

So Shelley's *Defence* once again uses the same image:

> Man is an instrument over which a series of external and internal impressions are driven, like the alternations of an ever-changing wind over an Aeolian Lyre. . . .

but he adds that the human being can adjust the sounds to harmony. In a later passage, which is well-known, he compares 'the mind in creation' to 'a fading coal, which some invisible influence, like an inconstant wind, awakens to transitory brightness'. We must try to find the source of this wind of inspiration.

Fingal's Cave

The sound produced by the Aeolian Harp was known as Nature's music; another way of listening to music produced by natural forces was to visit Fingal's Cave (131). This has already appeared, in the Gandy drawing (126), as an example of natural architecture, so the visit is doubly worth while.

The island of Staffa, meaning Staves or Columns, is off the west coast of Scotland, approximately eight miles north of Iona. The columns of

131 J. M. W. Turner, Fingal's Cave. Engraving by E. Goodall. Title page vignette from illustrated edition of Sir Walter Scott, The Lord of the Isles (1834).

basalt were created by volcanic action. This island is penetrated by caverns, one of which is called Fingal's Cave, after the bard in Macpherson's 'Ossian' poems; this cave is 227 feet long, and roughly 66 feet high, depending on the tides. The point of Gandy's drawing was that this natural phenomenon resembles human architecture; the columns appear to be very regular, usually hexagonal in shape, with horizontal jointing which adds to the effect of a stone building. It is a 'natural cathedral'.

The island was 'discovered' in the late eighteenth century, and was visited by Scott and Keats*. Scott contrasts the cave with the nearby church of Iona:

> Whereas to shame the temples decked
> By skill of earthly architect,
> Nature herself, it seemed, would raise
> A Minster to her Maker's praise!
> Not for a meaner use ascend
> Her columns, or her arches bend;
> Nor of a theme less solemn tells
> That mighty surge that ebbs and swells,
> And still, between each awful pause,
> From the high vault an answer draws,
> In varied tone prolonged and high,
> That mocks the organ's melody.
> Nor doth its entrance front in vain
> To old Iona's holy fane,
> That Nature's voice might seem to say,
> 'Well hast thou done, frail Child of clay!
> Thy humble powers that stately shrine
> Tasked high and hard—but witness mine!'
> *The Lord of the Isles* 4, x

The 'organ music' is a strange booming noise within the cavern, produced by the sea breaking through an underwater hole at the far end of the cave. Mendelssohn pays a musical tribute to this phenomenon in his *Hebrides* Overture, also known as *Fingal's Cave*; the opening ten bars were written immediately after his visit.

Notice how another chain of symbolism can be linked to this image: that of the cavern and the abyss of the unconscious. Thus, to recapitulate what must by now be obvious points, Shelley states that

> We are aware of evanescent visitations of thought and feeling. . . . It is as it were the interpenetration of a diviner nature through our own; but its footsteps are like those of wind over the sea, which the coming calm erases, and whose traces remain only, as on the wrinkled sand which paves it. . . . (Poetry) arrests the vanishing apparitions

and 'sends them forth'; otherwise there would be 'no portal of expression from the caverns of the spirit'.

---

*And also Wordsworth—see *Poems Composed or Suggested During a Tour in the Summer of 1833*: XXVII–XXXI.

Purgation Through Suffering

Keats described his impressions of Fingal's Cave in a letter to his brother Tom; he included a poem beginning — 'Not Aladdin Magian/Ever such a work began. . .' The important passage in the letter is this:

> The finest thing (on Staffa) is Fingal's Cave — it is entirely a hollowing out of Basalt Pillars. Suppose now the giants who rebelled against Jove had taken a whole Mass of black Columns and bound them together like bunches of matches — and then with immense Axes had make a cavern in the body of these columns. . . .

We are hardly surprised to find that there is a reference to a 'cathedral cavern' in *Hyperion*. It reappears in *The Fall of Hyperion*, this time in the introduction to the poem, where the poet is initiated into the mysteries of poetry:

> I look'd around upon the carved sides
> Of an old sanctuary with roof august,
> Builded so high, it seem'd that filmed clouds
> Might spread beneath, as o'er the stars of heaven;
> So old the place was, I remember'd none
> The like upon the Earth: what I had seen
> Of grey cathedrals, buttress'd walls, rent towers,
> The superannuations of sunk realms,
> Or Nature's rocks toil'd hard in waves and winds,
> Seem'd but the faulture of decrepit things
> To that eternal domed Monument.
>
> *The Fall of Hyperion* I, ll. 61–71

As the scene unfolds, however, it is blended with associations represented by the next picture. Blake's illustrations to Dante have already been used to show the descent into the underworld (109); in the *Purgatorio* Dante, accompanied in this illustration (132) by Virgil and Statius, has to ascend the mountain of Purgatory. Progress is slow because of the toil of climbing the steps; but at this point there is the additional barrier of the wall of fire: through this he must pass before he is allowed to meet Beatrice. The angel of the fire appears to be beckoning him to enter the flames.

In *The Fall of Hyperion*, which we know was influenced by Dante's poem, there is a remarkable resemblance to such a scene as this. A voice from behind the altar commands the poet:

> If thou canst not ascend
> These steps, die on that marble where thou art.

After climbing the steps and confronting 'the veiled shadow', he requests the Prophetess to 'purge off . . . my mind's film'.

> 'None can usurp this height', returned that shade,
> 'But those to whom the miseries of the world
> Are misery, and will not let them rest. . .'

132 William Blake, The Angel inviting Dante to enter the fire of Purgatory, *Illustrations to Dante's* Divine Comedy *no. 84 (1824–7). Pen and watercolour over pencil. Refers to* Purgatorio, *xxvii, lines 5–42.*

The figure 'parts the veils', and the poet is rewarded by

> A power within me of enormous ken
> To see as a god sees . . .

Similarly, in Shelley's *Defence*, poetry 'withdraws life's dark veil' and 'purges from our inward sight the film of familiarity which obscures from us the wonder of our being'.

The Lonely Tower

The Lonely Tower (133) is the greatest of Palmer's etchings. In discussing it we need to refer once again to Milton, who provided the initial inspiration —

> Or let my lamp at midnight hour,
> Be seen in some high lonely tower,
> Where I may oft outwatch the Bear,
> With thrice-great Hermes . . .
> *Il Penseroso*

and to Alexander Pope, who lived in a tower at Stanton Harcourt in Oxfordshire, while translating the fifth book of the *Iliad*. In this plate we are led to contemplate the mystery of poetry; the poet is seen as a special being. The watch-tower shows that he has gained a position of superior and elevated vision; he works late, and in solitude. Although the poets insist on the universality of poetry — Wordsworth, for example, said that 'Every man is a poet' — this image is the emblem of the lonely struggle which the poet must undergo, and which cuts him off from society.

The image occurs several times in the poetry of the period. Coleridge, for example, in his poem written after hearing Wordsworth read *The Prelude*, sees him as the poet of Hope,

> . . .calm and sure
> From the dread watch-tower of man's absolute self,
> With light unwaning on her eyes, to look
> Far on . . .

One of Shelley's heroes, Prince Athanase, in the poem of the same name,

> . . . sate
> Apart from men, as in a lonely tower,
> Pitying the tumult of their dark estate. . . .   (32–4)

Later in the same poem the Prince sits in a real tower with an aged teacher, and we are told that,

> The Balearic fisher, driven from shore
> . . .saw their lamp from Laian's turret gleam,
> Piercing the stormy darkness, like a star.   (187–90)

133 Samuel Palmer, The
Lonely Tower *(1879)*.
Etching, state IV.

Similarly, if we return to the detail of the etching, the two figures to the
right are lost in admiration; their darkness is in part illuminated by the
'star' of light in the tower: perhaps they think that the poet is working for
them.

Further examination of the picture reveals even more detail; it may be
necessary to use a magnifying glass. Between the two figures on the right
and the tower yawns a chasm, in which a stream can be distinguished; the
symbolism of this should now present no difficulty. There is an owl flying
out of it, presumably Pallas Athene's bird of wisdom. On the skyline can
be seen the trilithons of a 'Druidic temple' silhouetted against the moon.
In the wagon to the left a man is being conveyed up the road which leads
towards the tower, and another smaller person can be seen on the hillside
to the left of the tower.*

The Lonely Tower is a late etching by Palmer and takes us well beyond
our period. As a symbol of the poet's solitary quest for hidden knowledge
it reappears in the poetry of W.B. Yeats:

> We are on the bridge; that shadow is the tower,
> And the light proves that he is reading still.
> He has found, after the manner of his kind,
> Mere images; chosen this place to live in
> Because, it may be, of the candle-light
> From the far tower where Milton's Platonist
> Sat late, or Shelley's visionary prince:

*Identified by Mr Edward Malins as Milton's Bellman. See his *Samuel Palmer's Italian Honeymoon*,
pp. 120–2, for a very full discussion of this etching and other possible interpretations of its meaning.

The lonely light that Samuel Palmer engraved,
An image of mysterious wisdom won by toil...
The Phases of the Moon

Yeats, who was one of the earliest decipherers of Shelley's symbolism, said that in Shelley's poetry towers represent 'the mind looking outward upon men and things'. Be that as it may, implicit in the *Defence* is the teaching that all this labour will not be in vain: poets are 'the mirrors of the gigantic shadows which futurity casts upon the present; ... the trumpets which sing to battle and feel not what they inspire; the influence which is moved not, but moves.'

The Unbinding of Prometheus

So we return finally, to the Prometheus theme with which we began. One day the Titan, after much suffering, is to be liberated from his chains. In his *Prometheus Unbound* Shelley rejected the traditional story, which explained that the Titan was released after naming Thetis as the bride whose child would threaten Jupiter's empire: 'I was averse,' says Shelley in his Preface, 'from a catastrophe so feeble as that of reconciling the Champion with the Oppressor of mankind.' Instead, in Act III, Demogorgon, whom we have already encountered (p. 157), drags Jupiter down from Olympus into the abyss; this is followed by the unbinding of Prometheus, a task performed by Hercules (134). Shelley's verse drama ends with a vision of a regenerate world, a kind of secular Last Judgement.

134 Henry Fuseli, Prometheus Rescued by Heracles *(c. 1810). Pen and ink.*

135 William Blake, Glad Day *(c. 1794–6). Colour print.*

Blake, too, engraved several versions of a liberated figure, usually known as *Glad Day* (135). The reference to the coming of the dawn is from Shakespeare's *Romeo and Juliet*. On one version Blake added the words:

Albion rose from where he laboured at the Mill with Slaves
Giving himself for the Nations he danced the dance of Eternal Death.

So that, on this level, Albion is both a liberated and a sacrificial figure. The same gesture appears—back view—in a spectator of Christ's Crucifixion in another picture by Blake.

Both Blake and Shelley are piling significances onto their symbolic heroes, who are both, in a sense, self-portraits. We are witnessing the Triumph of the Imagination, and we are intended to feel that it is Poetry above all things which can save mankind. *The Defence of Poetry* concludes: 'Poets are the unacknowledged legislators of the world.'

How much any of the Romantic Poets lived up to such ideals may well be questioned by an uncommitted observer. But notice that Shelley's final words point beyond poetry and back into the world of men, as does the speech of Keats' Prophetess. If poets are really going to reassume the position they held in primitive society, if in fact we are going to take Shelley's words as having any literal meaning, then maybe poetry is not enough.

That Greece Might Still Be Free

It is 1824. Keats is dead; Shelley is dead; Wordsworth, Coleridge and
Blake are growing old. The scene is a marshy promontory near the town
of Missolonghi in Western Greece. Lord Byron, on the white horse, is seen
exercising his personal troop of Albanian Suliotes (136); we recall our
first picture of him (56), though this time he has designed a 'Homeric
Uniform' as more appropriate. He has come to Greece to stage-manage a
revolution against the Turks; in practice, it is difficult enough to maintain
peace among the three hundred soldiers who form his private army. After
two months he is bitterly disillusioned with them and threatens to send
them away.

The expected battles have not occurred; it is more important to try to
unite the quarrelling and divided factions among the Greeks. He still
talks with enthusiasm of the cause, but his health is rapidly deteriorating;
it is his will-power which keeps him constantly in the saddle. When we
look at him close to, we find him most himself in the company of his
Newfoundland dog; according to Parry, Byron was accustomed to say,
'Lyon, you are no rogue, Lyon. . . . Thou art more faithful than men,
Lyon, I trust thee more.' He was also heard to mutter a prophecy made to
him when he was a boy in Scotland—'Beware your thirty-seventh year.'
On the 19 April he died of a fever, a death hastened by the copious
bleeding prescribed by the doctors in attendance.

While there is no point in glamorizing this incident, we see here the

181

logical conclusion of Shelley's *Defence*. Though ineffective as a soldier, Byron truly became 'an unacknowledged legislator of the world.' By his death in Greece Byron did more good for the Greek cause than anything that his poetry alone could have achieved. Not only that, but all over Europe, as the nineteenth century wore on, Byron was remembered and imitated by poets and revolutionaries. One thinks of Pushkin and the Decembrists in Russia, Petöfi and the Hungarian revolt of 1848—even to this day Byron is the only English Romantic poet you can expect the average European to name.

He is also the only one of our poets to be commemorated in popular folk-poetry, the nearest equivalent to the primitive Bardic verse with which we began this chapter. Here is one of the Klephtic ballads circulated among the Greek soldiers after his death:

> A golden eagle flew high over Missolonghi,
> He looks to the right, he looks to the left,
>   he looks from on high at the castle.
> And with his sharp nails he lit on a frozen tomb.
>   Arise, my lord, awaken for it is noon.
> Awaken and don your arms, and take your pen,
> To write to the East, to tell to the West.
> Missolonghi is your tomb, one day you will arise
> With the leap of a deer, the pride of a lion,
> With the voice of a nightingale, to write the songs
> Which the enslaved sing, once they take up arms.

As he himself had said in 1821, in uncharacteristic and yet gnomic prophecy: 'There will be blood shed like water, and tears like mist; but the peoples will conquer in the end. I shall not live to see it, but I foresee it.'

Taking it further

A few years ago one could simply have instructed the average urban dweller to look no further than the centre of his own town for evidence of the continuing presence of the physical world of the early nineteenth century. But so much has changed with the needless destruction of old buildings to make way for car parks and supermarkets that it is very difficult to find a perfectly preserved time-capsule in which to obtain a true feeling for a period. Nevertheless, most towns will have a Regent Street or similar indicator, and thereafter an intelligent use of Pevsner's *Buildings of England* series will be found the best guide. One soon learns to look for characteristic lettering and street furniture.

In London, for example, a great deal can still be seen along the line of Nash's Regent Street and its extensions to North and South (137). John Nash was appointed to the service of the Crown in 1806; in 1811 his plan for the development of Regent's Park was accepted. Regent Street was driven between Soho and Mayfair, and, in effect, linked the Park with the Prince's residences, Carlton House, and later, Buckingham Palace. In doing this he provided the West End with a spine road. Though many of the original buildings have been drastically altered, if not demolished, the roads remain; and the curve of Regent Street, for example, is still to be seen (138). Though it is doubtful how much of this any particular Romantic poet actually saw, it should be possible for the reader of this book to make the imaginative leap between the architectural fantasies of John Martin and a well-angled view of Cumberland Terrace.

Another possibility, in a big town, is to wander in the inner suburbs, since development usually proceeds from the medieval or Tudor centre in concentric rings. In London, do not miss Hampstead, and Keats' House. Seaside towns were often built up from nothing in this period, and there is usually an opportunity for detective work behind the facade of bingo-hall and amusement arcade. Brighton, of course, is well worth a visit, including the Regent's pleasure-dome—the Pavilion. Finally, in any town or village, do not neglect the parish church, however genuinely medieval it may be. The walls are bound to house at least one plaque or monument of the period, with appropriate lettering and perhaps a verse.

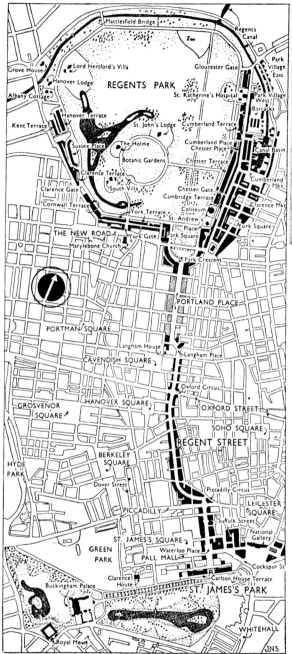

137 *Streets, squares and parks laid out by John Nash, 1811–35.*

138 T. H. Shepherd, The Quadrant, Regent Street, *London (1827). Ink.*

139 Thomas Banks,
Monument to Penelope
Boothby *(1791). In the*
church of St Oswald,
Ashbourne, Derbyshire.

In Ashbourne, Derbyshire, for example, you will find in the church this monument to Lady Penelope Boothby (139) which is said to have moved Queen Charlotte to tears. No other sculptor—among all the talented practitioners of this art in our period—can convey such a range of emotion, and it is appropriate that the repose of this monument should complement the energy of the *Falling Titan* (1) with which we began, both demonstrating the genius of Thomas Banks.

Books and Pictures

It is not really possible to provide any kind of general bibliography which would begin to do justice to any of the authors and artists discussed in these pages. The following book list gives a random selection of works which contain pictures or discuss images. Further help can be obtained from your local museum, library or art gallery.

M. H. Abrams, *The Mirror and the Lamp*, O.U.P., 1973.

John Barrell, *The Idea of Landscape and the Sense of Place 1730–1840*, C.U.P., 1972.

Asa Briggs (ed), *The Nineteenth Century*, Thames and Hudson, 1970.

Marcel Brion, *Romantic Art*, Thames and Hudson, 1960.

Kenneth Clark, *The Romantic Rebellion*, John Murray/Sotheby, 1973.

William Feaver, *The Art of John Martin*, O.U.P., 1975.

William Gaunt, *The Great Century of British Painting, Hogarth to Turner*, Phaidon, 1978.

Robert Gittings, *John Keats*, Heinemann, 1968.

Geoffrey Grigson, *The Romantics*, Routledge, 1942.

Martin Hardie, *Watercolour Painting in Britain Vol II: The Romantic Period*, Batsford, 1967.

E. J. Hobsbawm, *The Age of Revolution 1789–1848*, Weidenfeld and Nicolson, 1962.

Hugh Honour, *Romanticism*, Allen Lane, 1979.

Ian Jack, *Keats and the Mirror of Art*, O.U.P., 1967.

Francis D. Klingender, *Art and the Industrial Revolution*, Augustus M. Kelley, 1968.

Raymond Lister, *British Romantic Art*, Bell, 1973.

J. Livingston Lowes, *The Road to Xanadu*, Constable, 1966.

Rose Macaulay, *Pleasure of Ruins*, Weidenfeld and Nicolson, 1953.

Edward Malins, *English Landscaping and Literature, 1660–1840*, O.U.P., 1966.

Russell Noyes, *Wordsworth and the Art of Landscape*, Indiana U.P., 1968.

Nicholas Penny, *Church Monuments in Romantic England*, Yale, 1977.

J. B. Priestley, *The Prince of Pleasure*, Heinemann, 1969.

Peter Quennell, *Romantic England*, Weidenfeld and Nicolson, 1970.

J. Summerson, *Architecture in Britain, 1530–1830*, Penguin, 1969.

William Vaughan, *Romantic Art*, Thames and Hudson, 1978.

William Vaughan, *German Romantic Painting*, Yale, 1980.

R. J. White, *Waterloo to Peterloo*, Heinemann, 1954.

Acknowledgements

Keats Shelley Memorial Association, 26 Piazza di Spagna, Rome, for Joseph Severn, *Shelley Writing 'Prometheus Unbound' in the Baths of Caracalla, c.* 1820 (front endpaper), and photo 79; The Walker Art Gallery, Liverpool, for L. E. Fournier, *The Funeral of Shelley: The Last Rite at Viareggio,* 1889 (back endpaper), and photo 114; Royal Academy of Arts (1); The Syndics of Cambridge University Library (2, 37, 40, 42, 43, 55, 59, 63, 77, 122) Musée d'Art et d'Histoire, Geneva (3); Victoria and Albert Museum, London (4, 52, 96); Bibliothèque Nationale (5, 7, 80, 104, 123); the Trustees of the National Portrait Gallery, London (6, 31, 56, 69, 92); the Trustees of the British Museum (8, 49, 61, 70, 77, 78, 82, 87, 102, 119, 134, 135, 138); British Museum and the Mansell Collection (49); Fitzwilliam Museum, Cambridge (9, 17, 18, 88, 90, 113, 115); Fire Protection Association, London (10); Whitworth Art Gallery, University of Manchester (11, 44); Ann Ronan Picture Library (12, 33a); Gladstone Pottery Museum, Longton, Stoke on Trent (13); the Trustees of the Wedgwood Museum, Barlaston (14, 15, 16); Hodder and Stoughton Limited (19); Courtauld Institute of Art (118); Courtauld Institute of Art and the National Trust (20); Suffolk Record Office (21); the Trustees of the Tate Gallery (22, 34, 41, 64, 74, 85, 105, 109); Derby Museums and Art Gallery (24); P. L. Sully, Fellside Photos, Motherby (25); City of Bristol Museum and Art Gallery (26); Hamburger Kunsthalle (27, 39); Museum Folkwang Essen (28); Sir Gilbert Inglefield, G.B.E., T.D. (29); Allen Memorial Art Museum, Oberlin College, R. T. Miller Jnr Fund (30); Staatliche Kunstammlungen Dresden Gemaldegalerie Neue Meister (32); Manchester Public Libraries (33b); The Royal Institute of British Architects, London (35, 112); Museum der Bildenden Künste, Leipzig (36, 60); The National Maritime Museum, London (38); Munson-Williams-Proctor Institute, Utica, New York (45); Malmaison (46); Collection Liesville, Paris (48); Museo del Prado, Madrid (50, 53); Historisches Museum der Stadt Wien (51); Allen and Unwin (54, 137); Bodleian Library, Oxford (57, 71, 121, 125, 131, 136); Museum of Classical Archaeology, Cambridge (58); Birmingham Museums and Art Gallery (62, 65); Ashmolean Museum, Oxford (66, 67, 89, 91, 127, 133); Kunsthaus Zurich (68); Louvre, Paris (72, 73, 86, 120); Lady Lever Collection, Port Sunlight (75); Faringdon Collection, Buscot and The National Trust (81); the Trustees of the National Gallery (83, 93); Kunsthistorisches Museum, Vienna (84); Bedfordshire County Council (94); Cambridge University Press (95a, 95b); Pierpont Morgan Library, New York (97); British Library (98); Pinocoteca Vaticana, Rome (101); City of Manchester Public Library (103); Christopher J. Richards (106); Yale Center for British Art, Paul Mellon Collection (110); Southampton Art Gallery and Museums (111); New York Historical Society, New York City (124); the Trustees of the Sir John Soane's Museum, London (126); National Museum of Wales, Cardiff (128); Manchester Art Galleries (129); The Horniman Museum, London (130); National Gallery of Victoria, Melbourne (132); National Monuments Record (139). Photos 23 and 108 are reproduced from private collections. Photo 99 is reproduced by gracious permission of Her Majesty the Queen.

Index

Louis-Edouard Fournier
1889